Will —
Thank you for your

interest.

Best,

Mike Brady

Dreaming of Heroes

America and the Golden Age of College Football

By

Michael Grady

Dreaming of Heroes

ISBN 978-1-54398-742-3

Printed in USA

For Mom. I finally got to meet your Dad, and he is as amazing as you always said.

Contents

"Most of the USMA's greats have legends created about them long after their departure. – Cy was a legend while still a cadet."

Brig. General Charles W. G. Rich, Commandant of Cadets,
The United States Military Academy at West Point
August 1958

Prologue

At the time of his death in March of 1953, Jim Thorpe, a Native American, was widely recognized as the greatest American athlete of the twentieth century, ahead of such luminaries as Red "The Galloping Ghost" Grange and even the larger-than-life Babe Ruth. And yet, much to the dismay of his third wife and now widow, Patricia, Thorpe's own home state of Oklahoma would not erect a monument to honor its famous son.

Sensing an opportunity to boost the local economy, the small Pennsylvania town of Mauch Chunk offered to change its community name to "Jim Thorpe," erect a monument to the town's new namesake, and provide his final resting place.

Four years later, a group of five people stood together next to the great athlete's new resting place. Each held a metal cylinder roughly 12 inches tall and packed with soil from different corners of the Earth to spread upon Thorpe's new grave.

The first cylinder was held by Sadie Feder, an Indian princess from Oklahoma City and a former classmate of Thorpe's, who brought soil from the original Thorpe family farm in Prague, Oklahoma.

The second was held by John Lobert, a former teammate of Thorpe's from when he played professional baseball for the New York Giants. He spread a sample of soil from the famed Polo Grounds in New York where they had both played.

The third was in the possession of Leon Miller, a member of the faculty of the Community College of New York, who obtained and distributed soil from the Olympic Stadium in Stockholm, Sweden, where Thorpe had won the first pentathlon and decathlon of the modern Olympic era in 1912.

The fourth was carried by Peter Celac, a backfield teammate of Thorpe's from the Carlisle Indian School football team. His canister held soil from the Sac and Fox parade grounds in Oklahoma, the tribes of which Thorpe had been member.

And finally, sticking out a bit like a sore thumb, was a U.S. Army colonel in full military dress. The officer, who was currently stationed at the Army War College in Carlisle, Pennsylvania, had no obvious connection to Thorpe other than that his cylinder held soil from a Carlisle, Pennsylvania, football field where Thorpe had first played football as a student at the infamous Carlisle Indian School.

Thorpe himself had never served in the military, so one could be excused for wondering why there was a representative of the U.S. Army present at the dedication.

The answer, however, was fairly simple. Thorpe had exploded into the national consciousness as the nearly unstoppable backfield player for the Carlisle Indian School football team, then coached by the legendary Glenn "Pop" Warner. Further, he cemented his name with his play in a historic upset over the perennial football powerhouse Army in 1912—against a team that was captained by a young cadet named Dwight Eisenhower, who was now serving as president of the United States. The Army and the president sent a representative out of respect and recognition for that Army game and its importance in Thorpe's life.

While largely unknown, however, the colonel was well selected. Even though by 1957 his own story had already faded from the public consciousness, Col. Cyril J. Letzelter had been a college football superstar in his own right. He had played an important role in the sport both as a collegiate player and later as an assistant coach for the mighty Cadets of West Point. And importantly, unlike many others who made their mark on football at West Point and moved on to other things, Letzelter had remained with the military for his entire adult career. It also undoubtedly helped that Col. Letzelter was conveniently nearby, billeted to the U.S. Army War College at Carlisle Barracks.

FOURTEEN MONTHS LATER Col. Cyril Letzelter died suddenly of a heart attack at the comparatively young age of 51, just months before an anticipated promotion to brigadier general befitting his new post as the executive officer to the Army Chief of Staff for Intelligence at the Pentagon in Washington, D.C.

Unlike the 1920s and 1930s, when his sporting exploits were covered in newspapers from coast to coast; this time his death registered like most others—in his local and hometown newspapers, and in the alumni magazines and newsletters of the organizations of which he was a member.

It was in the West Point alumni magazine where Letzelter's longtime friend and the commandant of cadets at West Point at the time, Brigadier General Charles Rich, stepped forward to personally write Cyril Letzelter's obituary, pronouncing him a "legend" before he had ever stepped foot in the academy. This is obviously high praise from anyone, and even more so coming from one of the generals holding a leadership position at West Point.

This book is about the story behind those words. It's about the sport of football—about the unique role it played in capturing the nation's attention in the 1920s and in helping lift people like Cyril Letzelter out of lives destined for punishing work in the coal mines and steel mills of the Ohio Valley and beyond. It is also a window into the evolution of the game and the changes of the nation that occurred between Reconstruction and post–World War I America. In a sense, the game and the country went from unsteady experiments to fast-growing, powerful phenomena over the same period. And the youthful struggle on the gridiron during the period between the wars helped shape what we call the "Greatest Generation"—a generation of young men and women working toward a hopeful future, taking the risks they needed to take to get ahead, and sometimes being manipulated by stronger forces beyond their reach.

It is an American story.

In the Shreve High football stadium,
I think of Polacks nursing long beers in Tiltonsville,
And gray faces of Negroes in the blast furnace at Benwood,
And the ruptured night watchman of Wheeling Steel,
Dreaming of heroes.

All the proud fathers are ashamed to go home.
Their women cluck like starved pullets,
Dying for love.

Therefore,
Their sons grow suicidally beautiful
At the beginning of October,
And gallop terribly against each other's bodies.

"Autumn Begins in Martins Ferry, Ohio"

by James Wright

(*The Branch Will Not Break*, 1963)

From the Black Forest to the Ohio Valley

Long before the sport of football reached the Ohio Valley, the immigrants came. Many of them German and Swiss, they settled in the region in part because its rolling green hills and valleys reminded them of the Black Forest of central Europe they had once called home.

Monroe County, Ohio, located in the western foothills of the Appalachian Mountains, was created by the Ohio state legislature in 1813, early in the presidency of James Madison. Legend has it that the small community of Woodsfield was founded not long after by one Archibald Woods, who supposedly purchased a keg of brandy and offered free drinks to any man willing to help him remove trees from the main street. Within an afternoon, so they say, the road was clear. True or not, the story reflected the spirit of the new, tight-knit community that primarily provided the goods and services necessary for the farmers cultivating the surrounding countryside.

The German immigrants that helped settle Woodsfield came in a series of waves that began around 1820, a little more than a decade after the final collapse of the creaky Holy Roman Empire. The fall of the Empire had launched a period of large political upheaval in the Germanic states that reached its peak in 1848, during the March Revolution. Originally an attempt by the middle and lower classes to liberalize and nationalize the Germanic states, the rebellion ultimately failed, leaving the aristocracies in Austria and Prussia ascendant and liberal reformers fleeing the land.

The Grand Duchy of Baden had been one of the most liberal states during the revolution and was one of the last areas to be brought under control in 1849. After the defeat, the flight of the reformers launched the biggest wave of German immigrants to America between 1848 and 1880. Known as the "Forty-Eighters," it was this wave of immigration that brought the Letzelters to the United States from their homeland in the tiny Village of Schonau, tucked away in the hills of the Black Forest, not 30 miles from where the modern-day boundaries of Germany, France, and Switzerland all meet.

It was not long after the revolution was crushed that

Michael Letzelter made his first trip to America near the middle of the century. He stayed for two years until, confident he could build a life in the New World, he returned home for a time to arrange the relocation of his family. He returned to America for good in 1866—probably later than he had originally hoped, and no doubt delayed by the long American Civil War. His return brought not only himself and his wife but—for the most part—his children and their families as well, settling in Woodsfield.

Michael Letzelter and his wife Mary Magdeline Burkhardt — who immigrated to the United States in 1866 with his parents and siblings. They settled in Woodsfield, along with many other families from Schonau

Like most working-class Germans, Michael had learned a trade that he passed on to his sons. Upon arriving, the family set up a wagon-making and blacksmith shop in the local foundry on the east side of Woodsfield, where they advertised their skills in the complete manufacture of both farm and spring wagons, and their skill in the shoeing of horses. More importantly, they became the exclusive agents selling iron plows designed by the Oliver Iron Plow company. Using a newly patented "chilled" process to construct the plows, the South Bend, Indiana–based company overwhelmed its competition throughout the 1870s and 1880s, helping the Letzelters build a

Newspaper ad promoting the family business that appeared regularly in *The Spirit of Democracy*, the Woodsfield newspaper. This appeared in the Jan. 28, 1879 edition.

sustainable family business. They were also devout Roman Catholics and became founding members of St. Sylvester's Parish in Woodsfield, where Michael and many of his children and grandchildren worshiped and are buried.

MICHAEL WENDOLIN LETZELTER was the third of his name, the grandson of the first Michael Letzelter who emigrated to America in the mid-1800s. The sixth of eight children, he was raised in a German-speaking household and, with his siblings, quickly developed bilingual skills enabling him to communicate at home and in the world beyond. He and his two brothers, Charles and Joseph, set their gaze on the future and would eventually move away from the wagon-making tradition of their parents and grandparents, as this new generation embraced the new opportunities offered by the only place they ever knew as home.

Michael was the middle of the three boys, a young man with traditionally handsome features. He boasted a long angular face with a square jaw, reddish-brown hair, friendly eyes, and a slight curl to his hair when it grew too long. He was no older than the age of eighteen when he met the young girl who would steal his heart and change his life.

Michael Wendolin Letzelter and Mary Elizabeth "Mollie" Poulton, in approximately 1899

Mary Elizabeth Poulton, known as Mollie, was the same age as Michael. Born halfway across the state in the tiny village of Beaver, Ohio, she moved back with her family to nearby Belmont County—the place of her parents' marriage—in approximately 1890. Many of the Poulton family relatives lived throughout the Ohio Valley, mainly in Woodsfield and Wheeling, and Mollie's signature books from the era indicate that the family visited relatives often. Michael and Mollie probably first met during these visits, when Mollie's Catholic family would have attended St. Sylvester's for their Sunday services.

Precisely when they met is less certain. Mollie was a collector and keeper of signature books, a common practice of the era. The earliest one she received as a gift from her sister Emma in 1890 right before her ninth birthday. Her largest and last known signature book was given to her in 1894. The final inscription in her book was written on February 9, 1899. It read:

A basket of kisses
A peck of love
Give me some in return,
Or I'll give you the glove.

The author of that final entry was signed: "Mr. M. W. Letzelter." The remaining pages of the book were left blank as if there were no more signatures she needed to collect.

Their courtship would last seven years. While no specific stories remain, one can imagine a group of young boys and girls enjoying each other's company over time: Michael, his sister Laura, and their cousin Edith Schumacher teaming up with Mollie, her younger brother Martin (known as Bert), and Laura's boyfriend, John Caton—all of them near the same age, all of them spending a fair amount of time in Woodsfield.

One can imagine this because in that tiny town, on Tuesday, November 14, 1905, they got married. All six of them.

It must have been a remarkable event for such a small, close-knit community. The proceedings began early in the day when Father T. A. Goebel of St. Sylvester's Roman Catholic Church in Woodsfield presided over the marriages. The first joined Michael and Mollie in St. Sylvester's Church. Immediately after that, Father Goebel moved to the Church

Rectory, where he married Mollie's brother Bert Poulton and Edith Schumacher. He then traveled to the Letzelter family home where Michael's sister, Laura Letzelter, exchanged her vows with John Caton—a service that could not occur on the church grounds because Mr. Caton was not Catholic.

Mollie Letzelter holding her infant child Cyril Joseph in 1907

While the marriages were conducted separately, they were celebrated together, with all three couples sitting together for a formal portrait commemorating the rare event. One imagines that an event this unique likely touched the entire community. It also partially explains the need to preside over three different locations, as tiny St. Sylvester's Church could not hold the entire community.

After the festivities calmed down, Michael and Mollie, as well as Laura and John, settled into the Letzelter family residence at 143 Oak Lawn Avenue in Woodsfield with their recently widowed mother, and they began the process of building their own lives and families together. Within a year, they had their first child, a son, whom they named Cyril Joseph Letzelter.

THE STANDARD PRACTICE of people of German heritage was to learn a trade and pass it down through the generations. The Letzelter family had brought their trade of blacksmithing and wagon making with them to the United States. However, in this new world and new century, Michael and his older brother Charles saw the opportunity to do something different. In the shadow of the Second Industrial Revolution, with new manufacturers and factories popping up all over the valley, they turned their eye toward the growing field of industrial plumbing. Both of them were able to secure coveted apprenticeships with William Hare & Son Plumbers, Gas & Steam Fitters in Wheeling, West Virginia.

The training would take seven years to complete, but upon completion, Michael and Charles would be master plumbers with skills in high demand. Both his training and later work would require much time away in the Wheeling area working on large-scale jobs. While Michael worked, Mollie continued to live with her mother-in-law and began raising their young family. Over time more children arrived. Michael was born in 1908. Twin brothers Charles and Francis were born in 1910, but they were weak. Francis died within a day, while Charles fought for two weeks before expiring. Their youngest son, Richard, came in 1912.

Through it all Michael traveled to make money for the family, and Mollie stayed home with the children in Woodsfield. As the three boys grew, they became playmates, with older brother Cyril emerging as the natural leader. He was a charming boy who, like most elder siblings, had a strong sense of responsibility. The day his father came home to Mollie exclaiming of Cyril, "Mike, you've simply got to do something about this boy," he was greeted by the sight of a line of baby chicks lined up dead on the front porch. Little Cyril wasn't

being mean, though; he had accidentally killed them when he— trying to be helpful around the house—decided to give the new baby

Cyril (center) at play with brothers Richard (L) and Michael (R)

chickens a bath. The results were predictable.

Through his youth, Cyril was an attractive and easygoing boy, always ready with a smile, and always eager to play a pickup game of baseball on the nearby sandlot, or even that new and growing sport—football.

ON OCTOBER 30, 1916, a day before her thirty-fifth birthday, Mollie Letzelter wrote to her husband at the apartment he was keeping in Warwood, West Virginia. It was clear that their life was moving into a new and exciting stage. After eleven years of marriage that saw Mike on the road learning his trade and earning a living, they were finally set to settle down with his own business in a new home near downtown Akron, Ohio— just outside Cleveland and far from Woodsfield and Wheeling.

Mollie wrote longingly of how much they would be able to accomplish together once they were settled down, saying, "Just look how I have worried all these years and I feel like we will get along alright if only you will be with us for good." She spoke of their need to save "every cent" to make this new endeavor work. She nagged Mike to follow up on debts owed to him by friends and family and reminded him to send the goods needed for the new home.

She also explained to him that they had less than a month before the current tenant vacated the home. They were scheduled to take possession as early as November 23.

In a letter to her sister-in-law, Laura Caton, written the same day, she expressed some slight frustration with Mike for not having already arranged for the goods to be sent to Akron from Woodsfield. But her letter also showed she was in high spirits. She spoke of the fun she and the children were having since they were out of school during this transition period. She talked about how well her parents were treating them and mentioned that if Woodrow Wilson won reelection, her father was taking them all into Akron for a day of fun and a large celebratory dinner. She also spoke of the cold autumn weather and how she was already wearing a sweater given to her by her mother under her coat "for it is so cold when you drive."

She ended her letter relaying a message from four-year-old Richard to his cousin Rosemma asking her to come visit.

One week later, President Woodrow Wilson was narrowly reelected to a second term, with the state of Ohio providing the crucial votes securing the win. Despite the fact that neither Mollie nor her mother, as women, had the right to vote, she and her parents were undoubtedly thrilled. However, with such a short period of time to prepare for the move, it is unlikely that the celebratory trip to dinner in Akron occurred right away. Rather, one can imagine the frenzied pace Mollie worked to prepare for the big move.

At some point that fall, Mollie had moved north to her parents' residence at Franklin Township in Portage County, just outside their future home in Akron, where she waited anxiously for the goods Michael was sending from Woodsfield. The date of their relocation was fast approaching.

That November featured unseasonably cold weather—a factor that, along with the hectic pace preparing for the move, undoubtedly contributed to the cough Mollie developed that began to slow her down. The cough was followed by fatigue and then fever, and finally, by November 18, she was feeling poorly enough that she took to bed at her parents' house and was visited by the local doctor, F. A. Russell. He diagnosed her with bronchial pneumonia.

It would be twelve more years before penicillin was discovered, and decades more before its widespread use to treat bacterial infections. Despite Mollie's young age and vitality, the disease advanced quickly. Only five days later, at just thirty-five years of age, Mollie died. Her death came so quickly that her beloved Michael never made it back to her bedside.

Ironically, she died November 23—the very same day they were able to take possession of their first home. Their dreams died with her.

Evolution

It was only three years after the Letzelters arrived in the United States that the first organized game of American football occurred between two colleges: Rutgers and Princeton, in 1869. It took place at a turning point for the young nation.

Not only had the country just emerged from a traumatic and bloody civil war, but as the historian Taylor Branch said, the completion of the intercontinental railroad had, for the first time, left no visible frontiers to conquer. That, combined with the emergence of "intellectuals (who) believed that the sporting arena simulated an impending age of Darwinian struggle," led to a generation of leaders concerned about how best to prepare and toughen the country for the difficulties to come. It was in this environment that the men of the era began to view rugby-like games as a "toughening agent."

Such was the historical context in which the first intercollegiate football contest occurred. Rutgers (originally known as Queen's College) and Princeton (then known as the College of New Jersey) were just seventeen miles apart and had developed a fierce rivalry; as Wendy Plump described in *Princeton Magazine*:

> *On the side of rivalry, however, there was the fact that the town of Princeton had successfully outbid New Brunswick in 1753 for the final location of the College of New Jersey. There was the award of the state's Land Grant status to Rutgers in 1864, which Princeton had coveted for itself. There was a baseball game in 1866 in which Rutgers was thoroughly*

annihilated by Princeton. And there was the matter of the cannon wars, in which a disputed Revolutionary War cannon was repeatedly stolen and re-stolen by Princeton or Rutgers students vying for permanent possession. (The cannon today rests on Princeton's campus, sunk into several feet of concrete.)

Those battles having been settled, Rutgers and Princeton searched for new venues in which to express their growing and heated rivalry. It is generally understood that it was William Gummere of Princeton who suggested a series of three meetings to play football, with Rutgers hosting the first contest. As captain of the Rutgers team, William J. Leggett had the right to set the rules of play, and they adopted the rules of the London Football Association.

Under these regulations, the ball could not be carried at all but needed to be batted and kicked forward with feet, legs, arms, and even the sides of one's head.

Painting of the first Rutgers-Princeton game in 1869, painted by William Boyd, Rutgers Class of 1932

Princeton agreed to the terms, and so at 3:00 on the afternoon of November 6, 1869, two teams of twenty-five men took to a plot of land in New Brunswick, New Jersey, and faced off—more than double the number of players in a modern contest.

Neither team scored any touchdowns or field goals that day. In fact, neither type of scoring even existed. Instead, the

28

match was played as a "best of ten" series where each score—getting the ball successfully across the goal—represented a single game. So technically speaking, the first football game was in fact ten games, with Rutgers winning six to Princeton's four.

Not long after, other games began popping up at colleges across the East, usually with the home team determining the rules of play. A game generally adopted one of two distinct styles: either the European approach used in that first game at Rutgers or a style that featured ball carrying in a Rugby-like competition.

The differing approaches to the game led to the first ever meeting of schools, in October 1873, to discuss adopting uniform rules. That conference featured representatives of Yale, Columbia, Princeton, and Rutgers, and settled on rules resembling the soccer style of play. The other leading player in the East, Harvard, did not participate. Ultimately, home teams still set the final rules of the game.

This loose arrangement lasted for two years until, in 1875, two athletes from Princeton attended a game between Harvard and Yale. Harvard, as the home team, determined the game would be played rugby-style. They were so impressed with the game that they saw that they returned to their school and introduced the new style on their campus, where it also became popular.

The growing popularity of the rugby style led to another intercollegiate meeting at the Massasoit House in Springfield, Massachusetts, in late November 1876 to adopt new rules based on the code used by the Rugby Football Union from England. One key and unique difference was the replacement of a kicked goal with a touchdown as the primary means of scoring.

Three of the attending schools—Harvard, Princeton, and Columbia, went on to form the Intercollegiate Football Association, a very early forerunner to the modern National Collegiate Athletic Association. Yale, a previous adherent to the soccer style and a proponent of larger teams, opted not to join at first. Its resistance lasted three years, until 1879. Yale's

decision to relent was one of the most important moments in the early history of the sport, as it led to the full participation in the IFA of Yale's Walter

Massasoit House, home of many of the first meetings establishing the rules of American Football, photographed around 1882

Camp, the man who would single-handedly transform the game and eventually become known as the father of modern football.

WALTER CAMP CAME to Yale in 1876 and was an avid sportsman. During his time as an undergraduate, he earned varsity honors in every sport the school offered. When Yale finally joined the IFA, Camp became a regular participant in the numerous conventions held at the Massasoit House, where the rules of the game were continually debated and changed.

Once the IFA adopted the rugby-style play, one primary difference between the previous and new styles of play was the ability to carry, or possess, the ball while trying to advance. In rugby football, a player would advance the ball as far as possible until the accumulated effort and weight of the other team forced a player into submission, at which point the carrier would yell "DOWN!" and play would stop. After disentangling themselves, the men would restart play via a "scrummage," in which both teams would form an interlocking mass of people and appendages pressing against each other. Once set, the ball was thrown into the tunnel created by the players, and a fight for possession of the ball would begin anew.

Walter Camp pictured in 1910

Not incorrectly, Camp lamented the fact the game looked like little more than a disorganized mob.

His first proposal to change the rules was made in 1878—before Yale was even a member of the IFA—suggesting a reduction in active roster size from fifteen to eleven (team size had already been reduced by ten since the first game at Rutgers). His motion failed at first. However, in a pivotal meeting in 1880, this suggestion was adopted, along with several other new innovations that began to transform the game.

The most notable change that Camp successfully pushed in 1880 replaced the "scrummage" with a new "line of scrimmage." In this new scenario, once the person in possession of the ball yelled "DOWN," his team would maintain

31

possession of the ball. Rather than a new fight for possession, a player would "snap" the ball with his foot to a "quarterback," thus restarting play.

This change, combined with the removal of eight bodies from the field, had a dramatic effect on the game. On the one hand, the game was opened up, and new strategic opportunities presented themselves. However, it wasn't long before contests became little more than an attempt to maintain possession and run the clock down. What had promised to make the game more exciting was having the opposite effect.

It was Camp again who proposed the solution. At the 1882 rules meeting, he successfully argued for "down and distance" rules, where a team would be required to advance the ball a minimum of five yards in three plays.

In the space of three years, Camp's innovations had transformed the game from an unruly mob fighting for possession and advancement of the ball into a structured game with a line of scrimmage, a system of downs, a center, and a quarterback. While there was much more evolution to come, it is after the 1882 convention that we first begin to see a game that bears a resemblance to the modern game.

Nevertheless, football remained a small, relatively unknown game. As of 1880, only eight universities fielded intercollegiate teams. Growth and continued evolution, however, would come at a much faster pace.

AS THE NEW generations of the Letzelter family, and countless other immigrant families, began to set their roots in the New World, the new sport of football was also starting to take hold in the national consciousness. The game that had fielded eight intercollegiate teams in 1880 had grown exponentially to be adopted by thousands of colleges, high schools, and community clubs.

The University of Michigan had been the first team west of Pennsylvania to be formed in 1879. Two years later it became the first midwestern team to travel east for intercollegiate football, playing games at Harvard, Yale, and Princeton.

In short order, other teams began to pop up in the Midwest, with programs emerging at Northwestern, the University of Chicago, and the University of Minnesota. In 1895, this group of midwestern teams formed the first college football league: the Intercollegiate Conference of Faculty Representatives—also known as the Western Conference—a precursor to the current Big Ten. In 1902, the first postseason game was played in California, titled the Tournament East-West Game. It pitted Michigan (representing the East) against California's Stanford University. The annual contest eventually became "the Granddaddy of them All"—the Rose Bowl.

What is less known, however, is that college football's first intercollegiate conference emerged as a reaction to the growing violence of the game, particularly among the East Coast teams.

IN THE DECADE following the spate of reforms introduced by Walter Camp in the early 1880s, there was little change in the rules of the game itself. However, with the playing field now opened up and arranged around a system of downs and ball advancement, this decade of regulatory stability created the space for the development of new coaching and scoring strategies.

Many still saw football as an opportunity to prepare young men for a world defined by Darwinian struggle and survival of the fittest, so it should come as no surprise that military thinking began to play a role in the approach to the game. Nowhere was this clearer than in the development of one of the earliest and most electrifying of plays: the "flying wedge."

Lorin Deland was an unlikely suspect to develop football's most efficient and dangerous play. A Boston lawyer and a chess expert, Deland himself had never even seen a game until 1890. But once exposed to the sport, he became smitten, studying the rules of play and devising strategies for his enjoyment.

Deland had also been an amateur student of military strategy and had spent considerable time studying the tactics of Napoleon Bonaparte. It did not take long for Deland to find parallels to gridiron strategy. "'One of the chief points brought out by the great French General," Deland once observed, "was that if he could mass a large proportion of his troops and throw them against a weak point of the enemy, he could easily defeat that portion, and gaining their rear, create havoc with the rest."

Convinced he had a winning idea, Deland brought it to the coaches of the Harvard football team in 1892, which they then waited to use until the biggest game of the year, against archrival Yale.

Under the rules of the time, opening a half with a "kickoff" required no more than just tapping the ball with one's foot, thus making it live, and then picking up the ball and pitching it to a teammate. It is also important to note that in 1892, the game was still being played without protective equipment of any kind. There were no helmets, shoulder pads, face masks, or other protections that would become common years into the future.

It was in this context that Harvard introduced its secret new play. As the second half began, Harvard took to the field and immediately divided into two groups of five, each on opposite sidelines. Upon team captain Bernie Trafford's signal, the players began to move in unison, well before the ball was even put into play. As described by football historian Parke H. Davis in his 1911 book on the sport:

> *Each unit sprang forward, at first striding in unison, then sprinting obliquely toward the center of the field. Simultaneously, spectators leapt to their feet gasping.*
>
> *Restricted by the rules, Yale's front line nervously held its position. After amassing twenty yards at full velocity, the "flyers" fused at mid-field, forming a massive human arrow. Just then, Trafford pitched the ball back to his speedy halfback, Charlie Brewer. At that moment, one group of players executed a quarter turn, focusing the entire wedge toward Yale's right flank. Now both sides of the flying wedge pierced ahead at breakneck speed, attacking Yale's front line with great momentum. Brewer scampered behind the punishing wall, while Yale's brave defenders threw themselves into its dreadful path.*

And so it was that on the last Saturday before Thanksgiving in 1892, 21,500 spectators saw the game reach heretofore unseen levels of brutality. The strategy of Harvard was to focus all the momentum and energy of the flying wedge on a single Yale player, Alex Wallis, and mow him down. And mow him down they did. In an era where the average advance of a single play was two yards or less, Harvard's Brewer gained 20 yards. Overnight, college football transformed.

"It was a play that sent the football men who were spectators into raptures," according to the *Boston Herald*. The *New York Times* feigned excitement while expressing alarm over the increasing level of violence, "What a grand play! . . . a half ton of bone and muscle coming into collision with a man weighing 160 or 170 pounds. . . . A surgeon is called upon to attend to the wounded player, and the game continues with renewed brutality."

Upon the advent of the 1893 season, "mass-momentum plays," as they were called, were all the rage as teams across the east adapted the flying wedge for all purposes. Lorin Deland himself had used the off-season to develop 60 new momentum plays. The carnage was so great that newspapers began including injury reports as part of their regular football coverage.

After a full season of increased violence and injury, leaders both athletic and academic realized that changes needed to be made. Once again, the game turned to Walter Camp, now the head of the "Big Four" Football Rules Committee. Camp at first was reluctant to make significant changes, preferring to create only a "fair catch" rule to protect a punt receiver. But more important to Camp was the game he had helped to create.

Finally seeing not only the danger the play posed to individual players but the threat it posed to the sport itself,

Camp decreed the wedge an unsportsmanlike diversion from the traditional "rugby style" in which the game had its roots, and he proposed a series of new rules. The first new rule adopted for the 1894 season required the kickoff to travel at least 10 yards before it is in play unless touched by the opposing team.

While this eliminated Deland's original play, it did nothing to prevent other mass-momentum plays on both sides of the ball. So, after the 1894 season, the so-called Big Four met once again—this time with Princeton and Yale calling to adopt rules requiring at least seven players to remain stationary prior to the snap.

Harvard—the father of the mass-momentum play—was strongly opposed, as was Penn. The stalemate between the teams led to the dissolution of the Intercollegiate Football Association, and the teams once again reserved the right to play under their own preferred sets of rules.

Without a leadership entity in the east, a group of midwestern schools took the initiative to discuss the creation of a regional league that could address issues of violence and eligibility, as some schools were beginning to use non-student, semi-professional players. The result was the creation of the Western Conference in 1895.

Seeing the establishment of this new, upstart league to the west, Harvard and Penn quickly softened their opposition to rule changes and reformed the Big Four in 1896, and they agreed to the adoption of the seven-man fixed line. While mass-momentum plays could—and would—still be designed and executed with those players able to move, the flying wedge was dead, and the first intercollegiate conferences were born.

BY THE AUTUMN of 1905, President Theodore Roosevelt was facing a growing crisis in the world of intercollegiate football. The Progressive Era was fully underway in America, and the new "muckraking" style of journalism that helped usher in the era was a constant voice for change. The same crusading eye that had focused on poor working conditions, child labor, and consumer safety had recently set its sights on the corrupting influences present in the growing new industry of organized sport in America.

The small, strange collegiate game that boasted only eight programs at the end of the 1880s had undergone explosive growth over the previous two decades. By the turn of the century, there were an estimated 5,000 college, high school, and club teams operating across a 3,000-mile span of the United States. And as the popularity of the new sport grew, it was discovered to be a tremendous driver of revenue and prestige for local schools. From its very beginning, its ability to generate cash from gate receipts, program sales, advertising, merchandise, and souvenirs made football the cash cow for student-based athletic programs. Practically since its inception at the collegiate level to the modern day, football has been able to foot the bill for entire athletic programs at scores of institutions across the country.

But, as "muckrakers" instinctively knew, there's always a seedy underbelly where large amounts of cash are changing hands. And so in the summer of 1905, two nationally respected magazines, *McClure's* and *Collier's*, published extensive exposés on the darker side of the game. Their work shined sunlight on heretofore unknown practices such as providing exclusive academic considerations for players, hiring "ringers" to help ensure competitive teams, proselytizing (what we now call recruiting), and providing undisclosed financial aid to student athletes for tuition, room, and board.

They also exposed disturbing reports of players being coached to injure key players on opposing teams, which dovetailed with the growing concern over the ghastly toll the game was taking on players themselves. Still played with minimal protective gear at this point, the game had continued to rely on mass-momentum plays that technically got around the ban on the flying wedge yet still resulted in dangerous collisions, frequent injuries, and death with alarming regularity.

President Roosevelt, himself a former player and sports enthusiast, had been resisting calls to intervene and even abolish the game. However, in early October, he finally convened the heads of the three major schools—Harvard, Yale, and Princeton—securing a gentlemen's agreement to reinforce the standards of fair play and abide by agreed rules, which was hoped to at least cut back on the violence. At the time, the meeting and subsequent "agreement" were hailed as a breakthrough. The optimism would not last.

At the end of the season in late November, President Roosevelt received a report detailing the season's body count. The results were so shocking that, despite twenty-five years of increasing growth, profit, and popularity, the combination of shady practices and risk to human life seemed to hold the very real prospect that the game could be abolished.

It's not difficult to understand why. The report Roosevelt received was jaw-droppingly grotesque. A whopping seventy-one fatalities had occurred in games over the previous five years alone. While contemporary reports vary, the most conservative toll of the 1905 season was just as shocking: twelve players dead, eleven players with broken ribs, seven with broken legs, seven with broken collarbones, four with hips dislocated, two with fractured skulls, two with ruptured intestines, and one player with his eye gouged out. The list went on and on. Several students still hospitalized were in such poor condition that they were not expected to survive their injuries.

In many cases, the schools where students had died playing the game had voluntarily ended their programs. Others quickly joined the movement agitating for reform.

On the same day Roosevelt received his report, November 25, 1905, Union College of Schenectady, New York, faced off against New York University in the Bronx. Early in the game, during one of the many tussles, a nineteen-year-old by the name of Harold Moore, playing for the visitors, was inadvertently knocked out by one of his teammates. Although he was taken quickly via a fan's automobile to the nearest hospital, before nightfall Moore had died of a cerebral hemorrhage. On that same day, a high school player was killed on the field in Indiana, and in Missouri, another teenager was paralyzed from the neck down (and would die within the week). The news of all three events, along with reports of the season's overall toll, spread quickly across the news wires.

That same evening, Chancellor Henry McCracken of NYU—clearly upset over the events on his field earlier in the day—reached out to his counterpart at Harvard looking to initiate a meeting of the various college leaders to discuss

40

reform. Charles Eliot of Harvard, however, demurred, noting that major rule changes in football would ultimately need the blessing of Yale's Walter Camp, who still controlled the rules committee for the Big Four schools and was habitually resistant to change.

McCracken, however, was undeterred. As media coverage of the fateful events of that Saturday continued to spread, several key things occurred within a matter of days: First, the University of Pennsylvania announced plans to redouble reform efforts, specifically regarding the issues of player eligibility. McCracken scheduled a conference (without Harvard or Yale) in New York for attendees to consider rule changes and alternative sports to football.

But the biggest development was on the following Tuesday, when Columbia University announced its decision to abolish football and its threat to expel any students playing the game on their own initiative. This drastic action was driven not just by safety concerns but also by the desire to break the hold football had seized on the school consciousness. As one of Columbia's committee members involved in the decision stated clearly, "Only by such radical action can the university and college life be rid of an obsession which, it is believed, has become as hindersome to the great mass of students as it has proved itself harmful to academic standing and dangerous to human life."

Within a few days Walter Camp, who had thus far remained predictably silent, emerged to say that he agreed reforms were necessary and quickly suggested several ideas that had previously been offered and rejected. Among them was increasing to 10 yards the distance needed to achieve a first

41

down. However, Camp's focus was primarily to preserve as much of the current game as possible, and he remained resistant to the type of change that would fundamentally remake the game. As a result, 1906 began with two separate committees working independently on rules reform in advance of the coming season. One was Camp's committee, and the other was a new committee that had grown out of NYU's Chancellor McCracken's conference the previous December.

After months of working apart, by the end of 1906, the committees realized they had more to gain from working together and merged into an official organization: The Intercollegiate Athletic Association—later known as the NCAA. The new combined committee was responsible for determining and overseeing the new reforms.

The most notable change adopted was the introduction of the forward pass. Because it was introduced in an attempt to spread the playing field to reduce the scrums that seemed the source of most injuries, the original forward pass was much more limited than its modern form. Throws were limited to 20 yards or less, and they needed to be completed "outside of the tackles," or in the sideline zones outside the center of the field, and teams were penalized for incomplete passes. Camp's proposal to increase the first down requirement to 10 yards was also adopted, as well as the creation of a "neutral zone" between the two teams at the line of scrimmage, along with a significant expansion of penalties for unnecessary roughness, personal fouls, holding, and unsportsmanlike conduct.

The game remained violent, but the 1906 reforms were viewed as largely successful. While it took another six years before a program—Glenn "Pop" Warner's Carlisle Indian

School—was able to design an effective game plan that utilized the forward pass, and years more before it became a mainstay of the sport, the overall result was a more wide-open style of play that met with approval from the public. And slowly, over the coming decade, the introduction of leather helmets, shoulder pads, and other protective gear continued the ongoing efforts to address the rampant injuries of the sport. In the space of two years, football had transformed once again and made another subsequent leap in popularity.

Demographics and Destiny

The universities continued to tinker with this new American game supposedly aimed at developing the leaders of tomorrow into strong men ready to compete in a post-Darwinian world. At the same time, the German immigrants of the Ohio Valley were settling into their new homes, giving birth to a new generation of Americans poised to break free of the trade-based culture of their homeland.

They were not alone. In fact, not long before Cyril's ancestors were preparing to move their families from the mostly Catholic Grand Duchy of Baden to the United States, the Great Famine of 1840 struck Ireland, launching massive waves of Irish-Catholics across the Atlantic Ocean.

At the same time, modernization in Central Europe was upsetting the feudal, agrarian economy, with a new "bureaucratic" middle class taking root in the cities. The result was thousands upon thousands of peasants in the Germanic states and Poland forced from their land and fleeing to the New World. While the three different cultures came from different regions, spoke different languages, and traveled to the New World for different reasons, they predominately had one thing in common. These waves of immigrants were overwhelmingly Roman Catholic. Their movement across the Atlantic Ocean would upend the demographics and culture of the United States by the turn of the century.

Before 1845, Catholics were a small minority in America made up of mostly English Catholics who tended to be both professionally and socially accomplished. The estimated share of the population that was Catholic in 1850 was just 5 percent. By the turn of the century, they boasted a population of over 14 million people and had more than tripled their demographic footprint, comprising more than 17 percent of the country. During that same period, they went from a small religious minority to the largest single religious denomination in America.

Perhaps more importantly, the vast majority of new, Catholic immigrants were relatively uneducated working-class people willing to toil in punishing jobs for relatively low wages. As the Second Industrial Revolution powered America from an agrarian society to an international industrial powerhouse, a steady flow of immigrants filled the mines and the mills, serving as fuel for the engine of American progress.

This massive influx of immigration created political friction almost from the start. During the 1850s the Know-Nothing political movement exploded onto the scene fueled by fear of the growing political influence of new immigrant ethnicities and a deep distrust of the Roman Catholic Church. Officially called the American Party, the movement ran reactionary campaigns on a virulent anti-immigrant and anti-Catholic platform. Among other things, the party made the active disenfranchisement of these predominantly Catholic immigrants a major plank of its agenda, including efforts to restrict access to the ballot box from all except landowning males.

Over the next several decades, the spread of anti-Catholic rhetoric led to wild conspiracy theories. Stories spread of an imperialistic Pontiff in Rome plotting a takeover of the United States from within through the hierarchy of dioceses across the country. Rumors persisted of a Catholic militia made up of tens of thousands of Catholic men, calling themselves the Knights of Columbus, who were stockpiling arms and ammunition in the basements of their churches and awaiting orders from Rome.

Several statehouses even took steps to combat the "Catholic menace" by passing so-called "convent laws" that authorized warrantless searches of Catholic buildings to confiscate these mythical weapon stockpiles and rescue young women who had supposedly been seduced into the nunnery by alleged Catholic lies.

As crazy as it may sound, such beliefs were not a fringe element during this era. Anti-Catholic newspapers, magazines, and newsletters were widely popular—*The Jeffersonian* in Georgia and *The Menace* in Missouri each boasted subscription rates that dwarfed the largest newspapers in New York City and Chicago combined.

According to Ohio State University professor Sharon Davies, "Elections were won on promises to oust Catholics from positions of public trust. Only 'true Americans' should hold such positions, went the warning, not Catholics who were loyal first to their religious leader in Rome." Young priests who courageously stood up for their faith received death threats and occasionally lost their lives.

After the United States had entered World War I, a new ingredient of anti-German bigotry was mixed into the toxic stew of anti-Catholicism and race-based discrimination that had persisted and grown in the post–Civil War era.

Before 1917, many business, newspapers, churches, and schools operated in German, including in places like Cyril's hometown of Woodsfield. In fact, going back to the early eighteenth century, German was the second most widely spoken language in America. However, the onset of the Great War brought a significant political movement to suppress all things German. It was at this time that "frankfurters" became "hot dogs," laws were passed banning the use of German in legal documents, and even the act of speaking German was viewed as unpatriotic.

Nothing encapsulated the toxic atmosphere for Germans in America during this period more than the case of Robert Prager of Collinsville, Illinois. A year after the United States entered World War I, Prager, a coal miner, was rejected for membership in the United Mine Workers in nearby Maryville because of his German birth and the unjustified suspicion that he might be an enemy spy. Supposedly a stubborn man by nature, Prager returned the following day with a written document attacking those blocking his union membership, which he posted around town before returning home to Collinsville.

That night, he was confronted and captured in his home by a mob. He was quickly placed into protective custody by local police, but the crowd then overtook the jail, found Prager hiding within, and removed him. After giving him a moment to write a brief letter to his parents in Dresden, Germany, the mob hanged Prager in front of a crowd of 200 people. The following month, the ringleaders were found not guilty by a jury that barely took half an hour to deliberate.

To be sure, the Prager case is an extreme example, but the charged atmosphere in America caused a dramatic retreat in German heritage. Family names were changed. In the

47

Letzelters' home state of Ohio, the teaching of German as a foreign language was banned, even in private schools. In Cyril's home, where his father, aunts, and uncles all spoke fluent German, the use of the language both inside and outside the home ended abruptly, never to return. The impact was wide-ranging and lasting, as German never again approached its previous prominence as America's second language.

Despite the end of the war, the issue was exacerbated greatly in 1920 when Americans returned home from overseas. This was the dawning of the era of the Second Ku Klux Klan, and the group expanded dramatically when it rebranded itself as a "patriotic" fraternal organization dedicated to protecting America from Catholics, Jews, and other immigrant populations—particularly those of Germanic descent—that were still pouring into the nation. This new, second iteration of the Klan was seen as far more "respectable" than its previous form, attracting doctors, lawyers, judges, even members of the Protestant clergy, and seeing its greatest membership gains in the Midwest, outside the old South. President Woodrow Wilson, who already had a troubling record on race to begin with, refused publicly to condemn the new rise of the Klan.

As a person who was both Catholic and of German descent, there is no doubt that Cyril had to take his share of abuse. A letter that Cyril received from one of his most trusted family friends upon his graduation from high school made this point indisputably clear. Referencing treatment he faced as the star of his school's football team, he was encouraged to go forward and "show the same spirit and punch that has carried you through High School, despite the fact that bigots and fools have made the road doubly hard for you."

Fortunately, Cyril was lucky enough to be enveloped by the protective fraternity of American Catholics, and as he worked his way through high school and college, he and his fellow football-loving parishioners always had a special success story in which they could share pride.

Because when it came to anti-Catholic bigotry in particular, they all knew that despite those bigots, they could still claim spiritual ownership of the rise of what was fast becoming the most famous college football program in the nation. For many American Catholics, the football program at the University of Notre Dame led by Knute Rockne became a rallying point, capturing attention from coast to coast, including from young Cyril Letzelter.

IN 1896 THE University of Notre Dame, then barely fifty years old, made its first application for membership in the Western Conference. It was only a year after that league's formation. Rejected because the university's athletic governance and player eligibility rules were not well defined, Notre Dame quickly amended its athletic constitution to match the guidelines of other Western Conference schools and reapplied for admission in 1897. It was denied again, helping clarify that the Conference's original objection to Notre Dame's admission wasn't really about governance and rules after all.

In Murray Sperber's definitive work on the football program at Notre Dame, *Shake Down the Thunder*, he argues that the initial objections within the Western Conference were related not only to anti-Catholic contempt (though it was a significant factor) but also to a fundamental difference in the approach to higher education. As a parochial school that

49

emphasized religious training and open admissions, the Catholic institution was a cipher. The other midwestern colleges were unable to wrap their minds around the idea that a spiritual institution like Notre Dame, with a hierarchy that technically reached all the way to the Vatican, could have a faculty board with any realistic control over intercollegiate sports. In fact, the hierarchical structure of Notre Dame not only worked well but also helped insulate the school from the type of abuses with which the other schools were contending.

Nevertheless, the rejection by the Western Conference was a setback made all the worse as Notre Dame watched in-state rival Indiana and midwestern neighbor Iowa quickly gain admission to the league. For a school trying to set up an intercollegiate schedule, lack of access to a regional network of teams was a significant handicap to being taken seriously as a program. The Notre Dame squad was left to arrange competition with a combination of academic and nonacademic teams. In a telling anecdote, Sperber relates: "In 1901, the school opened the season against the South Bend Athletic Club, and Pat O'Dea, the Notre Dame coach, played for the opposition!"

Over the next several years, as Notre Dame struggled to build its program, the team began to travel farther for games. In 1904 they made their first trip west of the Mississippi to play the University of Kansas. They also had occasional success maintaining games against in-state rivals from the Western Conference—now called the Big Nine—Purdue and Indiana. Nevertheless, until 1908 the Catholic university struggled to schedule more than seven games consistently a season.

Things appeared to take a turn for the better in 1908 when Michigan, upset over changes in conference rules and

50

eligibility, temporarily abandoned the Big Nine. Out of necessity the Michigan program, led by an unabashed anti-Catholic by the name of Fielding Yost, reluctantly agreed to schedule Notre Dame in the interest of playing a complete schedule. It was the eighth time the two teams had met since 1889 when Michigan traveled to South Bend to teach the game to the new school. In 1908, Michigan dealt Notre Dame its only loss on the season, keeping its undefeated record intact. But for the Irish, the season was a success, with a nine-game schedule and an 8-1 record.

The following year, the Notre Dame team seemed to take its biggest steps yet into the upper ranks of college football. Not only did Michigan remain on the schedule, but the Catholics also added other significant opponents like Michigan Agricultural (now known as Michigan State) and the University of Pittsburgh. And the year was highlighted by Notre Dame's improbable undefeated season, marked by its stunning victory over Michigan in Ann Arbor—the biggest win to that point in the school's history. The only blemish on its record was a tie against Marquette in the season-ending game, which was enough to prevent a claim to the National Championship.

But that highlight would also lead to the most difficult times ahead for the upstart program. Michigan coach Fielding Yost seemed less upset about the loss itself than the fact that so many were taking Notre Dame seriously. He was embarrassed by the praise directed toward ND by none other than Walter Camp, who had attended the game in person and remarked positively about the strength of the Notre Dame running attack.

He was also furious with the overall news coverage suggesting that in beating Michigan, Notre Dame was a

51

program to be counted among the elite in the college ranks. Yost himself fumed, "We went into that game caring little about whether we won or lost," stating that for his squad, the event had been nothing more than a practice contest. His assertions led to even more critical coverage from midwestern sportswriters and deepened Yost's animosity toward the Catholic university.

After the success of 1909, Notre Dame pointed toward the following year with confidence and hope, only to learn the extent of the power that big-time college football programs could exercise. Not long after the end of the season, "poachers" from other, more established programs began to show up on campus dangling money and other incentives to entice the stars of the 1909 team to transfer. In fact, according to Sperber, the entire 1909 squad was given offers to move to Princeton.

In the end, a handful of top players took offers to transfer. Princeton scored star running back Pete Vaughn and lineman Luke Kelly, while several other players took offers from other schools, leaving the 1910 squad in a weaker position than expected. Another puzzling disappointment was that, despite Notre Dame's new profile, most of the big schools still would not schedule the university in 1910. The only significant competition for the coming year would be games with Michigan, Marquette, and Michigan Agricultural.

But the final indignity came in the final weeks of October when Michigan made a last-minute objection to the presence on the Irish roster of two players the university claimed were ineligible due to their having played previously for other colleges. Notre Dame was caught flat-footed by the charges, especially given that they had received advance assurances from Michigan in January 1910 that the players in question posed no problem.

The Irish made able defenses of their players, noting that their previous schooling was actually in preparatory schools and therefore should not count toward college eligibility, and they were able to point out that that Michigan had starters of their own that had played at other schools and supposedly used up their eligibility. Nevertheless, Yost remained unbowed. The vagueness and elasticity of eligibility rules at the time, along with the nation's general distrust of Catholics and immigrants, played to Yost's advantage. He was able to attack Notre Dame with impunity as a program that did not abide by the rules, while the Irish counter-claims gained little traction.

As letters between the school flew back and forth trying to resolve the impasse, Notre Dame got hammered in the court of public opinion. Less than twenty-four hours before game time, with the Notre Dame team already on their way to Ann Arbor, Yost canceled the contest. The move by the influential Michigan program, which at this point was again fully back into the fold of the Big Nine, had brought the upstart Notre Dame program to its knees. Not only had the Catholics been embarrassed by one of the great national football programs of the day, but they had been tarred publicly as cheaters.

In the wake of this, what had been a general anti-Catholic bias by the Western Conference that had existed since its inception was made into something much larger when Michigan's Yost worked overtime to institute a conference-wide boycott of Notre Dame, claiming that such programs were willing to "win at all costs." Yost's campaign was successful, as the following year past opponents such as Purdue, Michigan Agricultural, and even in-state rival Indiana all refused games with the Irish. A program that one year before had celebrated its greatest triumph now faced a future where the very survival of the program was in question.

THE BOYCOTT EXTENDED beyond football to all sports, putting Notre Dame in a horrible box. Locked out of competition with the major schools in its backyard, the university was only able to schedule substandard competition, which in turn drove the athletic department further and further in the red. Surprisingly, it was the sport of baseball that lit the way forward.

After the dismal 1911 football season, in which the program ran a $2,300 deficit, the athletic department immediately set to work trying to find ways to increase revenue. One idea was to send the baseball team on a spring road trip to the East Coast in 1912. Not only did this get the Catholics closer to the urban centers where so many immigrants and members of their faith lived, the road trip turned a profit of $860, suggesting a potential path forward.

At the beginning of December 1912, after another difficult football season, Notre Dame made the critical decision to hire its first full-time athletic director, Jesse Harper. He was given the charge to find a way out of the scheduling box imposed by the Big Nine boycott and get the overall athletic program at the university on solid financial footing. One of the first letters Harper sent was to the Army manager of athletics at West Point—one of the most powerful football programs in the East. Army, which had been cooperative with Notre Dame during the East Coast baseball tour in 1912 and was already working toward another matchup in 1913, quickly agreed. In a case of fortuitous timing, Yale had just unexpectedly decided to end its series with West Point, leaving an open spot on the academy's schedule for the coming season.

Coincidentally, West Point itself was under fire for its player eligibility guidelines that allowed any cadet to play sports during their time at the academy, a policy that allowed Army to field players who had already successfully attended, played, and graduated other universities. Notre Dame, desperate for real competition to reestablish their bona fides, had no objection to this policy.

Within the next three months Harper, copying the play out of baseball's handbook, had added games with Penn State in the east, the University of Texas in the south, and St. Louis University west of the Mississippi. The coming 1913 season would redefine Notre Dame forever, as a talented quarterback named Gus Dorias teamed up with an athletic left end named Knute Rockne to shock the world with a resounding 35-13 victory over Army, on its way to an undefeated, untied season. Notre Dame had not only broken out of the Big Nine's scheduling box, but it had proven itself all over the country, stacking up against the very best college football had to offer.

It was the beginning of Notre Dame's history of national scheduling, and it was driven almost entirely by the culmination of nearly two decades of anti-Catholic sentiment and the irrational dislike of the Catholic university driven relentlessly by Fielding Yost and the Big Nine. Despite the Catholics' successful season, Yost was able to hold the conference boycott together for another four years before

Wisconsin broke ranks and played the Irish in 1917. Others, such as Indiana, Michigan State, and Purdue, soon followed. But not Fielding Yost. He bitterly kept Michigan's boycott going for the rest of his years at the university. With the exception of two games during the depleted manpower days of World War II, the teams would not meet again until 1979.

It is evident in retrospect that the mystique of Notre Dame grew out of the school's reaction and survival instincts to the bigotry of the early twentieth century. And as its success grew, so too did its national support from Roman Catholics coast to coast. By the time Cyril was playing football for Martins Ferry, not only was Knute Rockne a living legend, he was a hero.

Autumn Begins in Martins Ferry

The sudden loss of Mollie Letzelter in 1916 was a staggering event for her husband and children. Overnight Michael and Mollie's relocation plans for Akron were sidelined. Michael's most immediate concern was how to ensure the proper raising of his three boys while still being able to earn his living as a journeyman plumber, with the required travel and extended absences that his livelihood entailed.

Unsurprisingly, Michael turned to his sister Laura and her husband, John Caton—with whom he and Mollie had shared their wedding day with so many years before—for help. Within weeks Michael and his boys had moved in with the Catons in their home on Wheeling Island, a large island situated in the center of the Ohio River between mainland Wheeling, West Virginia, and the Ohio border.

For Cyril, Michael's eldest child who turned ten years old just weeks after his mother's passing, the change must have been overwhelming at first. Not only was he without his mother, but the new living arrangement existed precisely so that his father could be absent for extended periods of time to earn a living. The addition of the Letzelters to the Caton household turned what had been a family of three into one of seven; vastly multiplying the essential activities necessary to run a household—and as the eldest child, Cyril was undoubtedly looked upon to step up and contribute more than ever before.

More than anything, however, the change in Cyril's surroundings had to come as a shock. His former home of

Woodsfield was a tiny, close-knit community atop one of the Appalachian foothills surrounded by forests. It had an economy dependent on the surrounding farming community and its related needs. Wheeling, on the other hand, was the metropolitan heart of the rapidly booming area along the Ohio River surrounded by mill towns that focused on the backbreaking work of digging coal and making steel. The mill communities presented most children with a grim, soot-stained, matter-of-fact glimpse of their future—one of long hours and hard labor and, with luck, a loving marriage and children. The communities themselves were efficient: houses in which to live, churches for worship, schools for education, general stores, and little else in the way of entertainment. The

Cyril as a young teenager.

era of widespread availability and use of automobiles wouldn't begin until after World War I, which meant that, given the modes of travel of the time, the forty-five-mile distance to Woodsfield might as well have been as far as the moon for young Cyril. But he adapted just the same.

Kids being kids, they rarely lack for imagination or ideas on how to entertain themselves. Throw a ball into the mix, and invariably a game of some sort gets underway. Throughout Cyril's youth, he was known as one of the kids always up for play. An agreeable boy, he was well liked and skilled enough to be a highly desired teammate. And for a little over three years, he remained on the island, attending the

58

Catholic school and always looking forward to those times when work allowed his father to be under the same roof with him.

However, the arrangement with his aunt and uncle was only temporary. As the majority of Michael's work continued to center on the booming Wheeling region, there was undoubtedly pressure for a more permanent living arrangement for the Letzelters. And so, in August of 1920, Michael Letzelter made what, in retrospect, was the most impactful decision in Cyril's life.

He rented a home and moved himself and his boys back to the Ohio side of the river—to Martins Ferry, the home of, as longtime Ohio football coach G. S. Yip Owens once said, "the most football crazy people I have ever seen in my life."

MARTINS FERRY LIKES to boast of its status of the first settlement in the state of Ohio. At its founding in 1779, during the Revolutionary War, expansion by colonists into the Ohio territory was still legally prohibited. Reinforcing the community's claim as the first settlement is the fact that it was Absalom Martin, a former captain in the Revolutionary War and one of the many surveyors of the Northwest Territory, who purchased the land that is now Martins Ferry in 1787. His purchase cemented his status as the first "legal" settler of the Ohio Territory. Two years later, he obtained the license to operate the ferryboat that provided the second half of the community's name.

Situated directly across the river from Wheeling, Martins Ferry was a critical outpost on the first national road constructed by the United States. This key route running through the mountains and connecting the Potomac and Ohio rivers, known as the Cumberland Road, ended at Wheeling. The crossing of the river into Martins Ferry became part of a well-worn path that had led later generations through the mountains of Appalachia to the fertile, midwestern prairie beyond.

As the new country moved through the First and Second Industrial Revolutions, the land bore added value from the vast stores of coal that lay beneath. The Ohio River gained importance as a critical commerce artery linking to the Great Lakes, and her water gave essential cooling and powering resources for the steel mills that began to dominate the valley. Before long, Martins Ferry was joined by an interconnected group of mill villages: Beech Bottom, Bellaire, Follansbee, Yorkville, and Bridgeport, not to mention Wheeling itself and more—all dedicated to the development of the ingredients of modern industry. Immigrants settled and earned a livelihood through the extraction and transportation of coal and the production of steel.

The jobs were honest and reliable. But they were also predictable and offered little opportunity to those generations who might dream of something more. Perhaps that's why the emerging world of organized sport—football, in particular—took such a hold on the imagination of the men in the Ohio Valley. Football offered distraction and, more importantly, hope that flowed from the fact that, from its very beginnings, football was connected to higher education. Across the nation in countless universities and high schools, football was like the old Cumberland Road: it was the path through the mountains, out of the valley, into the dream of the better life that lay beyond.

THERE ARE ONLY a small handful of high schools in the country that can boast of a football program with its roots in the nineteenth century, and Martins Ferry is one of the few. According to the well-respected local historian Annie Tanks, Martins Ferry High School's first football team (officially called the Charles R. Shreve High School, after the school's longtime former superintendent for the village) was fielded in November 1899. It was one of the six teams in the Central Ohio Valley Scholastic League, along with Wheeling, Bellaire, Moundsville, Wellsburg, Steubenville, and Cathedral (later Wheeling Central Catholic). It sounds more organized than it was.

For all the schools, football was a new project. And as they quickly learned, forming a league and creating a schedule are two entirely different processes. During that first year, not every team met on the gridiron, and in fact, there were so many open dates that weekends were sometimes filled playing other amateur teams from the area. At times, players were recruited from those who had dropped out of school to enter the workforce.

Ferry's first game was on the first Saturday of that November against the Bellaire Tigers. Again, according to Tanks, Bellaire scored a touchdown in the first half but apparently dropped the ball at some point. At this point, with football still a somewhat improvisational game, it was decided that the touchdown would stand, but Bellaire forfeited its right to kick for the extra point.

Trailing at halftime, Ferry made a drive all the way to the Bellaire 10-yard line before losing possession. However, a

Bellaire fumble gave the ball back, and Ferry scored but missed its point after attempt. The first game ended in a tie.

The next game against Cathedral High School occurred on Wheeling Island. Unfortunately, contemporaneous news accounts neglected to mention the score. The rest of the season was rather chaotic, as Tanks put it:

> *The third game was played at home on the Seabright field, ending in a victory for Ferry, 6-5. For the fourth game, the Ferry Merchants showed up, but the high school team did not, much to the Merchants' disappointment. The reporter scolded the high school team vigorously for their nonappearance. The fifth game was eagerly awaited, for either Martins Ferry or their opponent, Steubenville, could claim the league championship. To keep the crowd back in place, a wire was strung all around the field. Ferry trotted out on the field, and waited. And waited. This time, it was Steubenville that failed to turn up and the championship went to neither. Regretfully the high school found another Bellaire aggregation, the Buckeyes, for the closing game of the season.*

Future seasons proved more reliable and entertaining. After two more seasons, Ferry finally decided to name an official team coach. Dr. John Johns, who had recently returned from the University of Pennsylvania, became the high school's first football coach even though he was not a part of the faculty, and donated his time.

According to the history of Martins Ferry football, it wasn't until 1909 that football began to achieve a particular prominence compared to other sports. This new distinction came in large part because Hugh "Red" Smith, who became the school principal, had experience with the sport and became the community's biggest backer of the game.

In 1911, the school was without a faculty member able to coach the team, so once again it looked outside and named "Russ" Thompson, an alumnus, for the season. However, at this point, the popularity and prominence of the sport were growing so quickly that the Board of Education took the unprecedented step of hiring its first professional coach for the 1912 season, "Doe" Quailey.

Perhaps not coincidentally, 1912 ended up being Ferry's best season to date and further increased the popularity of the new sport. From that season on, the community of Martins Ferry built and earned a reputation of being unequaled in its passionate support for the boys of the local high school football team.

But with success came expectations, and poor results met with public disdain. No example stands out more than the description of the 1914 team in the annual school yearbook.

In the yearbook's section on athletics, year after year, football was prominently featured, with narrative and team photos and, in later years, individual photos. Football also received far more space than all other sports combined. But curiously, for the 1914 team, the opposite was true. While the other boys' and girls' sports each received their regular full-page photo and accompanying narrative, the page on football had no photo or artwork at all and was filled with nothing more than the following paragraph, typeset dead center on the page, under the script heading "Football":

The 1914 Football Team did not make as good a record as has been made by former teams from our high school, but this was due largely to the new material that had to be whipped into shape, and, worst of all, it was due to the lack of "spirit". The meaning of this little word seems hopelessly lost in our high school teams of late years, so let us hope that the 1915 team will have regained the pep characteristic of Ferry High's former teams. Fred Fest has been elected Captain of this years (1915) team and he is well qualified to fill the position; besides, there is splendid material left in the personages of Conway, Woods, Goff, Cropper, and others of last years team. So let us forget any personal feelings and get out and pull for dear old Ferry High's 1915 team.

The implication was both evident and harsh. The community had disowned the 1914 team, and the 1915 team was on notice: time to get back to playing real, Ferry football.

Whether it was the shaming or for other reasons, by 1920, the popularity of the sport had grown to the point where the revenues brought in by the program made it self-sustaining. Before that season, players had to provide their headgear and pads and shoes personally, rely on donated gear, or simply play only in the jersey, pants, and socks provided by the school.

The success grew with each year. In 1922 news reports from nearby Steubenville jealously noted that the Ferry program, now infamous for its community's support and pitched enthusiasm for the sport of football, had cleared an incredible $10,000 in gate receipts that year. Considering that the cost of a ticket to League Park in 1922 was just 25 cents, that figure seems almost impossible. But the financial report of the athletic boosters printed in the 1923 high school yearbook brought the intensity of Ferry football support into even sharper relief. While football brought in over $10,000, boys' basketball and baseball brought in $551 and $72 respectively. The people of Martins Ferry voted with their pocketbooks, and the results were nearly unanimous. Ferry was a football town, through and through.

The community reinvested the income into the football program. Throughout the 1920s, the program was able to run a profit of between $3,000 and $5,000 per season—the equivalent of $38,000 to $64,000 in 2019 dollars. By mid-decade the program built up a surplus of $15,000, which, combined with an additional $35,000 in community donations, allowed the school to construct a proper football field, a total expenditure that, in today's dollars, would represent an investment of nearly $640,000.

The athletic fund surplus was used in 1925 to buy the so-called Carmichael property, which had been a cornfield but was near the rapidly growing industrial section of town, close to the riverfront. By Thanksgiving, a 300-foot-long grandstand made of concrete, metal, and wood had been erected on the site. Additional sections of grandstand were added over the next several years so that, within a few seasons, Carmichael Field was capable of seating more than 3,700 fans.

The field was first christened Carmichael Field and was later immortalized as the "Shreve High football stadium" by the Pulitzer Prize–winning poet James Wright. Those glory years between 1920 and 1924, when the program began to make real money—enough money to build a massive stadium that still stands today—coincided closely with the years that Cyril

Letzelter rose to become, unquestionably, the most spectacular high school player in Martins Ferry and, arguably, the Ohio Valley. It is surely a stretch to suggest that the new field was "the house that Cyril Letzelter built," but there is no doubt he played a critical part.

Relationships

The tradition of earning a varsity letter dates back to 1865, when the Harvard baseball team added an embroidered letter "H" to their jersey and allowed the team captain to designate certain players as eligible to keep the jersey at the end of the season as a reward for playing in the most important games. By the mid-1920s, earning a varsity letter was a staple of sporting programs of all types and at all academic levels.

Receiving the letter, however, or even playing on the varsity team was a privilege reserved for upperclassmen. And, in the case of football especially, freshmen were not permitted to play with their older schoolmates. So, despite starting high school in Martins Ferry in 1921, Cyril was not eligible to play football until the following year.

He was undoubtedly aware of the intensity surrounding football in Martins Ferry before he went out for the team in 1922. Even so, he had to be impressed by the local booster clubs plan to celebrate the start of the season by calling on the entire community to meet downtown at the corner of First and Walnut streets so they could parade together to that Saturday afternoon's game as a unit, led by the high school band.

In trying out for the team, Cyril was faced with another reality peculiar to football of the era. Unlike how coaches approach position assignments today, stacking the line of scrimmage with the heaviest, strongest players. in the 1920s— at least in Martins Ferry—the bigger and stronger players were reserved for the backfield positions, while younger players paid their dues on the line. As a result, Letzelter started his football career as a right guard, duking it out on the line of scrimmage. There's no indication that this disappointed him. In fact, the school yearbook write-up on Cyril especially noted the fourteen-year-old boy's "Letz go and get 'em spirit." In fact, he appeared to excel in the unglamorous role. The yearbook pointed out that he possessed uncharacteristic speed and a toughness that made him a capable run blocker on offense.

Reinforcing the hometown write-up in the annual is the fact that he received his first All-Valley honors in his role as a sophomore lineman. According to the description of his selection, he made an impression as being arguably the best guard in the Valley, saying, "Between McMasters of Bellaire and Letzelter, less yards were gained via them than any two guards in the valley." Cyril was already getting notice.

However, there was little indication yet of the playmaker he would become. In fact, the most significant developments of the 1922 season were the friendships Cyril built with his teammates, most notably a fellow lineman and elder classmate by the name of Kenneth Williams.

Kenneth was the son of Welsh immigrants who had arrived in Martins Ferry at the turn of the century. While his older siblings were born in their home village of Pontardawe, in the county of Glanmorganshire, Wales, Kenneth and his younger sisters were born in the United States. As a result, this created the curious, but not uncommon, situation where the younger half of an immigrant family had full citizenship rights by birth, while the elder members of the family would have to be naturalized to obtain citizenship.

Kenneth and Cyril became fast friends, and Cyril became a regular fixture in the Williams home. It led to his taking notice of Ken's youngest sister, Ethel, who was two years his junior.

While no stories or letters exist explaining how Cyril and Ethel became so close, it's not hard to imagine that a contributing factor was that both had experienced the profound loss of their mother figures and undoubtedly still felt the sting of grief. However, while Cyril's loss had occurred nearly six years prior, in Ethel's case, the wounds were still fresh.

Years before, Ethel's oldest sister, Gwenllian, was promised a trip back to Wales upon her graduation from high school. In 1911, Gwen, along with her second-cousin Lillian (who lived just across the river in West Virginia), traveled back to

Kenneth Williams, Cyril's high school friend and future brother-in-law, in Ferry football uniform

Pontardawe to visit friends and family left behind.

Unfortunately, after what was to have been an exciting trip before starting her own life, Gwenllian returned home to devastating news. While she had been overseas, her mother, Elizabeth, three months pregnant, had suffered a miscarriage that cost both mother and child their lives. Upon Gwen's return to the United States, she was almost immediately informed of two things. First, that her mother had died in her absence, and second, that as the eldest, she was expected to step in and take over her mother's role running the household and raising the younger children.

There is no doubt that Gwen, undoubtedly feeling the loss of her mother, also greatly resented the new responsibilities placed upon her shoulders. While her plans at that point were unknown, they almost certainly did not include putting her life on hold for ten more years washing clothes by hand with a washboard, scrubbing floors, cooking meals, and raising her younger brother and three little sisters. Whatever her dreams, they died with her mother as she was an ocean away, enjoying her last free moments of youth.

Regardless of how she felt about it, Gwenllian did her duty. For the next decade she became a mother and a house servant, and by all accounts she did an able job. Unsurprisingly, young Ethel, barely three when her mother passed, became particularly attached to her elder sister. And under her care, Ethel grew from toddler to a teenager. By her sophomore year, she had matured into a stunning young lady with a cherub-like face and deep brown eyes; and at just 4 feet 11 inches tall, she counted as one of the taller Williams girls as well. It's easy to see why she caught Cyril's eye.

Not that there were many opportunities for romance, however. Ethel's father, Samuel, was a very proper man who was self-conscious of his Welsh accent even though he spoke

Ethel Williams, Cyril's future wife, in 1924

both impeccable English and Welsh. He was also a godly man, and the social life for young Ethel and her sisters consisted of Sunday mornings, Sunday evenings, and Wednesday evenings at the local Presbyterian church.

This was the normal state of affairs until one afternoon in the fall of 1924 when Ethel, then a sophomore, returned home from school to find Gwenllian had disappeared without a trace. After ten years filling her mother's shoes, Gwen packed up and left without warning and never to return, having fled to finally begin her own life. While one can understand Gwen's motivations, Ethel took the loss particularly hard. Gwen was the only mother she could remember. Worse, this wasn't a death but an abandonment, and it left deep scars.

It was in the wake of this upheaval that Ethel and Cyril fell for each other. While it is uncertain how big a role their common background of loss played in the early days of their relationship, it's not difficult to imagine Cyril comforting Ethel's pain with stories of how he had persevered himself in the face of unimaginable loss.

The bond they built in the early 1920s lasted the rest of their lives. And as Cyril rose in prominence as a football star, Ethel was his most enthusiastic cheerleader.

The Breakout Season

As the 1923–24 school year dawned, sixteen-year-old Cyril not only earned a coveted place in the Ferry backfield as a fullback, but he also was recognized for his kicking ability and was given the responsibility for the team's PAT attempts (extra points), field goals, and, occasionally, punting. Also, as was the norm for that time period, he played both sides of the ball as a member of Ferry's defensive backfield. His selection for these roles would give him ample opportunity to be in the middle of the action, but it appears that Ferry coach Earl Loucks did not realize at the start of the season just what he had on his hands.

It didn't take long to find out. During the season opener, against Canonsburg, Ferry fell by the paltry score of 3-6. But the story of the game, at least according to the newspapers, was the new member of the backfield who had a dominant game on both sides of the ball. Reports gushed, saying that "Letzelter played a whale of a game from the backfield, a position new to him." While he did not score a touchdown, the team, led by his close friend Ken Williams at quarterback, got into position once for Cyril to score Ferry's only points via field goal. Beyond that, his influence was mostly felt on defense where, in an era where forward passes were still primarily used as "gimmick" plays, Letzelter still managed to intercept two.

The following week at Zanesville again saw Cyril make his offensive contributions primarily with his kicking foot, scoring a field goal and a PAT for a total of four points as the team romped to a 23-0 win. While the real star of that game was his future brother-in-law Ken Williams, who scored two touchdowns, almost as noteworthy were the reports of confusion reigning on the field because the teams wore similar colored uniforms. Unlike modern football, where regulation dictates dark or light jersey colors based on the hosting team, such rules didn't exist at this time. So Ferry's purple jerseys and white pants were often mixed up with the Zanesville blue and white jerseys. Nevertheless, Ferry persevered.

It wasn't until the following week against Bridgeport, played at home in Martins Ferry's League Park, that Cyril got his first real taste of football glory. In what the newspapers described as one of the hardest-fought football games in years, Ferry ended halftime trailing by a score of 7-0. In a match Ferry was expected to win easily, it was only Cyril's exemplary work as the team punter that had kept the game close to that point.

The second half was equally hard fought, with running back Raymond Swaim able to finally get Ferry on the board with a touchdown late in the third period. Letzelter's extra point tied the game, setting up Cy's heroics where, as the clock was ticking down, he kicked a field goal at a sharp angle from the 25-yard line. It was no gimme, but his ability to convert was the game-winning play that allowed Ferry to eke out the win.

After a month playing a key role in the backfield, Cyril had been a reliable and consistent performer, but not particularly a standout at this point. But that was about to change.

ON SATURDAY, OCTOBER 13, 1923, Martins Ferry was in the middle of an unseasonably hot Indian summer. It was the fifth straight day of above 70-degree temperatures, and on this particular afternoon, the mercury would peak at an August-like 84 degrees, one of the hottest days of the autumn heat wave.

For football players in the early 1920s the protective gear

Cyril, during the 1923 season in his Ferry uniform

worn by players was both limited by modern standards and voluntary. However, because of the financial success of the Ferry program, the entire team was completely equipped with a full set of jerseys, pads, and helmets. The gear of this era was made of thick leather and was heavier and warmer than the plastic-based equipment used by future generations. And while technically air conditioning had already been invented, there were no systems built to cool sidelines as we see today, no indoor stadiums, no retractable roofs.

Football was a game where the elements in which you played were sometimes as important as the players themselves.

It was on this day that Westinghouse Tech High School traveled from Pittsburgh, Pennsylvania, to Martins Ferry to square off in League Park, the local baseball field that was converted each fall into a football field.

The park itself seemed impossibly small. Stretching the gridiron from the third baseline to the outfield left barely enough space for each team's benches and cheerleaders. And while the modest-sized grandstand provided a good amount of seating, the majority of spectators would still be packed around the field looking in through the chain-linked fence. Some would be sitting in their cars, others climbing into the trees to get a view of the action.

The blazing heat, combined with Westinghouse's daunting 15-pound-per-man advantage over Ferry, quickly turned the game into a punishing defensive struggle, with Ferry holding onto a slim 3-0 lead going into the final minutes of the contest. The only score had come from the toe of yet another Letzelter field goal.

However, as the clock was winding down, Westinghouse was making a final, dramatic push for a win. With both teams withering in the heat, the guests on League field began to leverage their considerable size advantage, battering their way downfield to a point where it seemed all but certain that their size and strength would carry them to at least a tie, if not an outright victory.

Finally advancing the ball deep into Ferry territory against a spent defense, Tech began the pivotal series with a first and goal on the Ferry 10-yard line, already well within the distance for a game-tying field goal. But they had time to go for the win, so they lined up once again.

Three straight times, Westinghouse tried to power the ball up the middle, and three straight times the exhausted and inspiring Ferry boys held. Running out of chances, Westinghouse was faced with a choice: they could play for the tie and kick a field goal, or they could make one last effort for a touchdown. Surprisingly to the crowd present, Westinghouse chose the latter, and the two teams lined up for the play that was certain to decide the game.

As the ball was hiked to the Westinghouse quarterback, the Ferry defense and fans present were shocked again as the offense dropped back for a rare forward pass. And then, as the contemporary accounts described it, "Pittsburgh passed the ball, and the crowd held its breath. Suddenly, a purple and white uniform was seen to emerge from the melee and started streaking toward the south goal."

Cyril Letzelter had unbelievably intercepted the ball at the 4-yard line and found the strength and speed to outrun the entire Westinghouse team to score a heretofore unheard-of 96-yard pick for a touchdown. Again, as described at the time, "It was the most sensational and spectacular play ever pulled on a Martins Ferry field and sent some 2,500 fans into hysterics."

At a time when the forward pass was still in limited use, Cyril managed to position himself to turn the tactic against Westinghouse, and in the process, he performed a feat that seemed so amazing to football watchers at the time that the sportswriters of the area could cite no similar precedent. His achievement was immediately touted as an All-Valley record and resulted in his name being splashed across the top of every sports page in the valley. In almost every story, the outcome of the game itself took a backseat to the description of Letzelter's incredible run.

Midway through the 1923 season, Martins Ferry had found its star.

WHILE CYRIL HAD been an important and productive cog in the Ferry machine, the Westinghouse game represented a turning point. He was now the clear star of the team; all eyes were now trained on Ferry's playmaker, their scorer, and their defensive leader. Now under an ever-brightening spotlight, he rose again and again to meet the challenge.

The next week, against Marietta, Ferry faced what was considered the most formidable team they would meet all year. And even though Ferry lost the game narrowly by a score of 13-20, once again Cyril shined. His running from the backfield was consistent and impressive, with individual runs of 15, 14, and 20 yards each. He also accounted for 100 percent of Ferry's scoring that afternoon. His first touchdown came on offense with a pair of back-to-back runs that covered 15 yards and crossed the goal. His second came on defense as he scooped up a fumble and ran it 60 yards back for a touchdown—his second straight game with a dramatic score from the defensive side of the ball. Not only that, Letzelter added two more interceptions to his growing season total. It was a performance that single-handedly kept Ferry in the game.

Cyril showed no sign of letting up the following week against Adena, another home game. Cyril scored 15 points on two touchdowns, and three successful extra point attempts. Over a stretch of three amazing games, Letzelter had notched nearly 70 percent of the points scored by Martins Ferry and proved himself a force to be reckoned with on both sides of the ball.

AFTER AN EXTRA week layoff, Martins Ferry began to prepare for the biggest game of the year against archrival Bellaire. To this day it remains one of the oldest rivalries in all of American football, dating back 111 years. In 1923, the importance of this game was already well established. Both teams routinely took steps to protect their practices from spies the week before the match, with contemporary accounts noting the Martins Ferry police's role in establishing a perimeter around League Park to protect the Ferrians from prying eyes.

This year, the game was to be played at Riverview Park in Bellaire in front of a crowd of 7,000. Bellaire wore their traditional red-and-white jerseys compared to the purple-and-white of Martins Ferry. Ferry also entered the game as an underdog, as the team's senior halfback, Raymond Swaim, was sidelined with a damaged shoulder he had injured in the contest against Adena two weeks prior.

Nevertheless, the consensus was that Martins Ferry outplayed Bellaire for the first two and a half quarters, as the Ferry defense completely stopped the ground attack of Bellaire star Obie Miles. However, perhaps due to their shorthanded backfield, Ferry was also unable to score. In response, Bellaire switched tactics and came out at halftime launching an aerial attack punctuated by plunging runs to finally twice force themselves across the goal line.

The only score by Ferry came at the hands of Letzelter, who, guarding Obie Miles, once again intercepted a pass intended for his rival, broke two tackles, and took the ball in for a touchdown. Perhaps fatigued by the run, Letzelter was unable to convert the point-after attempt. Bellaire won 13-6, but a buzz remained around the play of Letzelter.

In fact, the buzz stayed swirling around Cyril for the rest of the season, because in game after game, he never failed to impress. Against Erie Central, he led Ferry to a 24-0 win on the strength of three rushing touchdowns. Against Shadyside, it was "only the crashing drives of Letzelter and Siandru that saved the Purple because the Shadyside ends were able to move almost unopposed." Ferry notched another 19-0 win.

He maintained his momentum through the season-ending game against Linsley, where he led Ferry to a 26-2 win by scoring a rushing touchdown on offense, two PATs on special teams, and another defensive touchdown on a fumble recovery that he ran back 57 yards for the score. It was his fifth defensive touchdown off a turnover that season, and a large exclamation point on the end of his season.

The retrospective of that 1923 season is astonishing. Martins Ferry led the Ohio Valley in scoring with a total of 188 points. Of that total, 102 of those points were scored by Letzelter alone. During the season he had scored 14 touchdowns, 3 field goals, and 9 PATs, and accounted for well over half of the Martins Ferry offensive juggernaut. As far as can be determined, he was named to every single All-Valley team in the region, and in most cases judged to be the captain. Which was fitting, because the Ferrians also decided the same at the end of their season, electing Cyril to be team captain the following year.

In the space of three short months, Cyril Letzelter emerged from the hyper-competitive world of Ohio Valley football as perhaps its best player. By season's end, it was evident to all that Cyril would be a player in high demand at the collegiate level, providing him the priceless opportunity to become the first member of his family to go to college.

To get there, Cyril would need to navigate the shadowy, unregulated world of college football recruiting as it existed in the 1920s. Fortunately, help was on the way.

The Fixers

By 1924 what had started as a resurgence in football as the soldiers of the Great War returned home had turned into a full-blown explosion. From coast to coast, games were attracting record crowds. Universities were investing in massive new stadiums to expand their football profits and prestige. Sportswriters filled endless column space with breathless stories of gridiron battle, often veering into the realm of hagiography.

There is none more famous than the writings of Grantland Rice of the *New York Herald Tribune* who, in describing Knute Rockne's dominant 1924 Irish backfield as "the Four Horsemen," described a quartet of young men just a few years removed from high school as equal to the vengeance of God:

> *Outlined against a blue-gray October sky, the Four Horsemen rode again. In dramatic lore they are known as Famine, Pestilence, Destruction and Death. These are only aliases. Their real names are Stuhldreher, Miller, Crowley and Layden. They formed the crest of the South Bend cyclone before which another fighting Army football team was swept over the precipice at the Polo Grounds yesterday afternoon as 55,000 spectators peered down on the bewildering panorama spread on the green plain below. ("The Four Horsemen" by Grantland Rice,* New York Herald Tribune, *October 18, 1924)*

By the mid-1920s it was inescapably clear that collegiate football was becoming more than just a proving ground for the men expected to lead the future. Football was now a big business, with alumni to satisfy, expenses to cover, seats to fill, and newspapers to sell—all of which brought intense pressure for schools produce winning programs. Even so, mostly hidden from public view was the intense, competitive, and occasionally ethically questionable fight to attract football talent that confronted a top high school prospect like Cyril Letzelter as he entered his senior year at Martins Ferry in 1924.

Unlike the modern era where a clear set of rules and penalties exist regarding athlete recruitment, in the 1920s there were no national guidelines governing the use of scholarships or other incentives to attract players. Instead, different conferences adhered to different rules, some codified in writing, others assumed in the spirit of fair play.

This sense of "fair play" was so expected by the general public that when stories of perceived ethical lapses happened to make news, it was the very act of recruitment itself that was condemned. In fact, it was rarely referred to as "recruiting" at all, as that was a term that carried certain positive connotations. "Proselytizing," as it was then called, more accurately reflected the current point of view that hustling to acquire talented players was the equivalent of selling out.

Additionally, there was little to fear in the way of sanctions. For example, throughout most of the 1920s, it was common knowledge throughout the Big Ten that the University of Iowa's program was operating a slush fund to pay its athletes. Yet it wasn't until the end of the decade when Northwestern forced the Big Ten to take the extreme act of cutting off athletic relations with Iowa that the university was compelled to begin cleaning up the program.

At the center of it all were networks of fans, alumni, and even sportswriters who took up unofficial roles serving as part of the national network of "fixers" that kept an eye out for local talent, and who served as a vital communication link between their communities and the major college programs. At times the methods of fixers could be questionable, but their efforts opened the door to a higher education for thousands of American boys from working-class families.

The Ohio Valley, being a hotbed of football activity, had its share of these fixers. Two, in particular, would play critical roles in Cyril Letzelter's college football experience: J. Francis Mullaney of Martins Ferry and J. Francis Wallace of Bellaire.

JOHN FRANCIS "BUD" Mullaney was an entrepreneur with a deep devotion to his church and a great love of sports. A devout Roman Catholic who attended St. Mary's Parish on Fourth Street in downtown Martins Ferry, he resided most of his adult life on the same street, in homes that were never more than three blocks from his church.

It's not clear exactly when Bud first got to know Cyril Letzelter and his family, but it seems likely that the acquaintance dates to the arrival of Michael Letzelter and his boys in Martins Ferry in late 1920, as they would surely have met on Sundays at that church. What is certain is that, after that breakout 1923 season, Mullaney took an intense and active interest in the boys' future.

Part of this was undoubtedly due to Mullaney's reputation as a highly connected sports promoter in the Ohio

Valley. But what cannot be overlooked is the importance of their shared Roman Catholic faith and the determination of American Catholics to stand together as decades of bigotry reached an apex in the 1920s that would last the decade.

For his day job, Mullaney was a superintendent of the nearby Yorkville Tin Plant, a position he held in no small part due to his role inventing and patenting an automatic tin plate doubler that allowed the Yorkville plant to increase its production by 25 percent. But his passion was sports, and he was a well-known promoter in the Ohio Valley.

He once famously set up an exhibition baseball game for the Philadelphia Nationals in Martins Ferry only to see the event canceled due to rain. Being the savvy operator that he was, however, he had taken out a $1,000 rain insurance policy to protect his expenditures in setting the event up. As the rain began to fall, Mullaney walked out to the mound and set a dishpan to collect water and record the amount of rain. As he sat alone in the grandstands, watching the pan, three young boys ran onto the field attempting to upend the collector. Mullaney charged the field, and the contents of the container were saved. As 4:00 p.m. arrived, the expiration time of the insurance policy, Mullaney produced the proof of 2/10 of an inch of rain, and he collected his $1,000 claim.

In retrospect, however, nothing cements Mullaney's status as the "go-to" guy for football in the Ohio Valley more than his January 1920 meeting with Joe Carr, another Ohio sports enthusiast who was then trying to build a professional football league.

For over 10 years, Carr had been fielding and coaching a professional team of Columbus-area railroad workers known as the Columbus Panhandles. The railroad worker connection was central in Carr's ability to keep this rare professional team afloat. They largely scheduled road games based on existing train routes, allowing him to avoid travel and lodging costs. Road games also meant he encountered minimal costs to rent venues in which to play. As a result, the Panhandles had extremely low overhead. That, combined with Carr's exceptional skills as a promoter, led the Panhandles to be one of the most famous teams in the country at that time.

By 1920, Carr had set out to meet with local sports leaders with the idea of building a regional, professional league with potential franchises in seven other Ohio communities and one in Fort Wayne, Indiana. His first stop was to make the pilgrimage south via train to meet with his old friend and fellow member of the Catholic fraternity, J. F. Mullaney, in Martins Ferry.

Carr's meeting with Mullaney was intended in part to build media attention for his nascent effort. Within the year Carr had successfully joined others and helped to launch the American Professional Football Association, naming sports icon Jim Thorpe as its first president. The following year, Carr himself took the reins of the organization and renamed it the National Football League. He served as the league's commissioner until 1939 and to this day is considered the father of professional football, an accomplishment for Carr that began with that first trip to see Bud Mullaney.

Carr made that trip not just because they shared a common faith and friendship, and not just because the Ohio Valley was football territory, but because when it came to sports, the Ohio Valley was Bud Mullaney territory.

DURING THIS ERA, at the close of every high school football season in the Ohio Valley, area newspapers became inundated with reader submissions sharing their mythical "All-Valley Eleven," selecting the makeup of their dream team of local gridiron talent. The qualifications allowing you to submit and expect publication of your proposed team appeared to require little more than paper, a pen, and perhaps a postage stamp and envelope.

But even in this area, Mullaney stood apart from the average local boosters. Where most submissions were given an inch or two of column space and were probably used to fill gaps in sports-page layouts, Mullaney's seasonal selections were given so much space and attention that one might have thought Zeus himself had descended from Mount Olympus to render judgment. His 1923 All-Valley submission warranted a banner headline seven columns wide, and his loquacious prose used a whopping 56-plus inches of column space, not counting photos and graphics. Unquestionably, Mullaney's selections were both well respected and hotly anticipated.

One of the reasons his choices were given such importance was the evident diligence and thought he put into the process. Using the ample space provided by the newspaper, Mullaney would first spend thousands of words expounding on the qualities that defined an elite player and academic leader. It was only after having taken the time to place his selections in their proper context that he would reveal his position-by-position picks.

Mullaney also took advantage of this significant platform to share how he felt about football's unique role in providing an opportunity for countless boys to achieve a higher education. As he wrote in December of 1924:

Why do great throngs cheer themselves hoarse over football classics? Why do men who have never passed the eighth grade or who have never seen the inside of a college hall go out and cheer and cheer again? Why do alumni vie with undergraduates in exultation? Because football is on the level more so that any other sport in America. It is the one sport that furnishes a stepping stone to a higher education, if the young man is wise enough to grasp the opportunity shining before him! As long as our high schools turn out good, clean, high-minded boys well versed in the fundamentals of a higher learning, it is bound to follow that colleges and universities will uphold this standard. (Wheeling Daily Times, December 6, 1924)

It was in Mullaney's 1923 review that we saw our first indication that he believed he had found something special in sixteen-year-old Cyril Letzelter. Having carefully observed his breakout season, he not only named him the captain of his 1923 All-Valley team, but he also wrote of him:

We have placed Letzelter at fullback and made him captain of the team because he was the one player in the valley who continually had his head up. This style of player makes him an ideal captain. He speared a pass and ran 96 yards for a touchdown against Westinghouse Tech. Picked up loose balls

86

against Bellaire, Marietta, and Linsley and ran for touchdowns. Against Bridgeport, with the score tied and his team absolutely shot, insofar as advancing the ball was concerned, he stood on the twenty-five-yard line and from a difficult angle booted over the three points that won for his team. Against Linsley, with Swearengen the regular kicker horde combat, he took up the kicking burden on a field that was a sea of sticky mud and made five boots that averaged 41 yards. A Neimec couldn't have done better. He played in every game, never was taken out on account of injuries and winning or losing he always wore a smile that put pep and determination in his teammates. And so he played his part, better than the best.

From that point on, Letzelter became an ongoing project for Mullaney. He was going to ensure that Cyril was "wise enough to grasp the opportunity shining before him." As the 1924 season approached, Mullaney quickly shifted his focus from that of an active observer to a shaper of events.

J. FRANCIS WALLACE was a native of the football-rich Ohio Valley. His hometown of Bellaire was the archrival of its nearby neighbor to the north, Martins Ferry. The son of Irish immigrants, Wallace, like so many others, went to work after high school for the same Wheeling Steel Corporation that owned the Yorkville Tin Plant that was operated by Bud Mullaney. He was one of eight children, and in 1919 his siblings pooled their resources to send him to University of Notre Dame to study journalism.

He could not have foreseen how advantageous this opportunity would be. Upon his arrival, the new football coach, Knute Rockne, had just started the practice of plucking students from the journalism program to serve as his press aide. This innovation set Rockne apart from other coaches of the era and spoke to Rockne's gift for using the media to promote the image and stature of the Notre Dame football program.

In 1920, Wallace's freshman year, Rockne chose a senior by the name of Arch Ward to be his first press assistant. It was Ward, who went on to become sports editor of the *Chicago Tribune*, who is recognized as the first sportswriter to refer to the Notre Dame football team as the "Fighting Irish" in print. However, after Ward's senior year, Rockne had to replace his assistant. Thus, he tapped sophomore Francis Wallace as his replacement, which was Wallace's first step toward becoming, as Notre Dame historian Murray Sperber put it, "Rockne's Boswell"—his living biographer.

Initially, Wallace's job in this role was to create profiles of Rockne's star players and feed that information to the press. Over the course of the 1921 season, his mandate would come to include sending an endless flow of information, from speculation about upcoming games to the latest betting information and estimated point spreads. Sperber reported of Wallace that "the ND coach recognized his talent and co-opted him by appointing him Ward's successor. For three seasons, Rockne taught the student his methods." He became one of Rockne's most trusted aides.

For example, in 1922, when the school administration was exploring the idea of issuing varsity letters to the school's debate team, Rockne and Wallace, feeling varsity letters should be reserved for actual sports, worked together to strangle the idea before it ever caught traction. The two worked together to write a story that ridiculed the idea, describing the debaters wearing "ruffles and laces" and lining up in "fierce formations." After Wallace published the story in the *Scholastic*, the student body effectively laughed the idea out of existence.

In truth, however, Wallace's greatest assistance to Rockne came after his graduation, as he was one of the most prominent sportswriters to help build the mythical backstory of Notre Dame.

Shortly after his graduation, Wallace became a sportswriter in New York and carefully covered his alma mater and mentor. One of his first projects was to try to develop a nickname for the Notre Dame program that would stick. While his predecessor Ward had been the first to coin the term "Fighting Irish" in print, it had not yet caught on. Wallace tested out different nicknames, such as "The Blue Comets," before he settled on exclusively using the term "Fighting Irish" from his perch as a sportswriter for the *New York Post* in 1925. By 1927, with Wallace continuing the promotion to the much larger audience of the New York *Daily News*, the nickname became so widespread that the university gave its official blessing, and the nickname finally stuck.

Wallace also played an integral role in the creation of the mythical George Gipp story, reporting Rockne's inspiring halftime speech to his 1928 team, facing a tough game against a powerful Army squad, charging his men to "Win one for the Gipper!"

However, a lesser-known but far more important collaboration with Rockne occurred in 1927. The previous year, concerns about collegiate proselytizing had become so intense that the Carnegie Foundation for the Advancement of Teaching commissioned a study on American college athletics that would ultimately take more than three years to complete. The report would eventually rock the college football world in late 1929 by alleging that "one out of every seven engaged in intercollegiate competition" was "subsidized to a point bordering on 'professionalism.'"

The clamor for reform became such that Rockne felt less and less inclined to share his actual beliefs on the matter publicly. As a result, he turned to his former aide to become his anonymous mouthpiece. By 1927, Wallace had been covering the sports beat in America's biggest city for four years and was writing for the New York *Daily News*. He had achieved enough credibility that when Wallace submitted and published an essay in *Scribner's Magazine,* entitled "The Hypocrisy of College Football Reform," it was noticed and clearly impacted the debate. But what was not known until decades later, when Sperber unearthed evidence from the Notre Dame Archives, was that that piece, along with others written by Wallace pushing back against the reform movement, was, in fact, a collaboration with Rockne himself.

Not only had Rockne suggested the idea of writing such pieces to Wallace, but he reviewed early drafts, made changes, and even added material. Through Wallace, Rockne was able to loudly and secretly attack the proposed reforms of the Big Ten—who had once again rejected a Notre Dame bid for membership the year before—as "naive, wrongheaded, and hypocritical."

While Rockne, like most coaches of the era, relied on a strong network of friends and alumni to acquire talent, as the reform movement continued to grow, the coach carefully limited his contact to a smaller group of trusted friends. Among these close, trusted friends was Francis Wallace himself, who, as a native of Bellaire who returned to the area often, had become Rockne's eyes and ears in the Ohio Valley, searching for prospects and helping ease their path to Notre Dame. In one missive, Wallace wrote to Rockne of a prospect "as good as Neimec" who nonetheless needed more schooling to be able to succeed at Notre Dame. Wallace even went so far as to wonder if arrangements could be made for a local Alderman to foot the bill for an additional year of prep school for the prospect.

Rockne's faith was well placed, as neither Wallace or any of his other trusted "bird-dogs" ever revealed Rockne's recruitment and subsidization methods, thereby supporting the myth that Rockne ran an exceptionally clean program.

Even after Rockne's tragic death in a plane crash in March 1931, Wallace continued his efforts on behalf of ND, still being referred to as part of the "Notre Dame Press Network." And long after Rockne's death, he was still said to serve as a "bird-dog" in the Ohio Valley, hunting for football talent and often paying the cost to send prospects to South Bend.

Opportunity Shining

As Cyril approached his final year of high school football, it was apparent to all that he possessed the talent and ability to take advantage of that "shining opportunity" to leverage his athletic prowess into a higher education. It would mean, however, that Cyril and his family would need to navigate the shadowy, unregulated world of college football recruitment as it existed in the mid-1920s. Fortunately, with Mullaney as the guardian angel on his shoulder, he had ample help at his disposal, and his mentor wasted no time in getting to work on his behalf.

For much of the decade, Harrisburg Tech High School in Pennsylvania was considered one of the outstanding high school programs in the country. And since as early as 1921, Harrisburg had indicated its openness to playing Ferry if the Ohio team were willing to make the trip. And therein lay the rub. Harrisburg was 250 miles to the east. Any matchup would require a cost and time commitment far beyond what was normal for most high schools, even Martins Ferry.

However, Mullaney, the steel magnate, began working his contacts in the state of Pennsylvania to set up this very unusual matchup for the 1924 team. Mullaney took the lead on arranging a long weekend trip for the football team to travel by rail via Pullman car to Harrisburg to play a game and then continue to Washington, D.C., for a sightseeing experience. The game was set to take place in mid-October.

Playing in Harrisburg would provide a showcase for interested programs in the East to see Cyril play in person. We also know from correspondence between Cy and Mullaney that, at least for Mullaney, this was his top priority. Not only did he stress to Cyril the importance of the game, he likely worked to ensure "bird-dogs" from various colleges would be in the stands that day.

However, before he could get to Harrisburg, Cyril would first have to lead his team as its captain through the first stretch of the season.

COACH EARL LOUCKS stepped down at the end of the 1923 season and was replaced by Glenn "Yip" Owens, who was new to Martins Ferry but not new to football. Even so, after his first few days in town, he exclaimed that he had never experienced a community so crazy for football. This first impression was no doubt reinforced when preseason tryouts for the squad occurred, and 129 boys showed up hoping to make the team.

Letzelter had been elected at the end of the prior season to serve as the captain and had first met with Owens when he arrived in town. As the season approached, he helped lead daily practices at League Park to prepare. However, shortly before the season opener, he suffered an injury to his shoulder that would leave him unable to play.

So Captain Letzelter was forced to watch from the sidelines for his team's first game against Warwood, which Ferry won 12-3. The inability to play was so frustrating for Cyril that the next week, against St. Clairsville, he vigorously protested Owens's decision to keep him on the bench again to protect his injured wing. It was undoubtedly a good decision by the coach, however, as Ferry rolled over its opponent by a score of 33-0, and Owens had pulled the entire first team from the game midway through the second quarter.

Leading into their first October game against Tridelphia, the team switched their practice venue from their longtime location at League Park to the still-unfinished Carmichael Field, located down in the river floodplain amongst the steel mills and coal mines that dotted the western shore of the Ohio. Owens made the move because, despite not being completed, the field perimeter included a fence with lockable gates, and he had noticed that advance scouts from Harrisburg had begun to arrive to investigate his squad. He used the incomplete stadium to stymie the prying eyes of their biggest opponent of the year.

As the Tridelphia game approached, advance newspaper coverage reported definitively that Letzelter once again would be benched due to his injury. This time, however, Cyril's protestations did not fall on deaf ears, and Owens let him play.

Despite only accounting for two extra points, newspapers hailed Letzelter's return as his greatest game yet. While that description was clearly hyperbolic, it is true that he impressed observers especially in light of his injured status. In limited action, he cut loose with runs of 35 and 18 yards and accounted for a total of ten first downs in a narrow, 14-0 win for Ferry.

Only one game remained on the schedule for Cyril to return to full strength before the critical matchup in Harrisburg—another home game against Wellsville. It was described as the marquee matchup of the week in the Ohio Valley, as Wellsville was returning a squad that had only lost one player from the team that held mighty Bellaire scoreless on their home field the previous season.

Cy wasted no time getting started. After Wellsville's first possession had ended with a punt, he took the first snap 17 yards to the opposing 28-yard line. Two plays later, he broke a 15-yard run, setting up his teammate Clem Siandru for the first touchdown of the day.

It was the beginning of a massacre. Right as the second quarter was beginning, with Wellsville controlling their ball from their own 29-yard line, they fumbled the ball. Letzelter pounced, grabbing the pigskin on the run and carrying the ball 29 yards for his first touchdown of the day.

Later that same quarter, Ferry received possession again deep in Wellsville territory. Letzelter contributed runs of 10 and 2 yards on his way to scoring his second touchdown. It was not even halftime, and Ferry led 19-0 with Cyril having been the driving force behind every score.

As the teams returned from halftime, Cyril began lining up to take snaps as quarterback. On his first possession, he connected with Siandru for a 30-yard pass. He later added an 8-yard run to get Ferry inside the 10-yard line, setting up fellow backfielder Jack Burd to get the short-yardage touchdown.

On their next possession, Ferry intercepted Wellsville at the Ferry 40-yard line. Letzelter went to work and marched his team downfield, uncorking a 28-yard run on his way to his third touchdown of the day. It was only the middle of the third quarter, and Ferry had built a 51-6 lead. At this point, Owens then pulled his entire starting team to rest. It was evident to everyone that their captain was back at full strength.

AS THE SUN came up on Friday, October 17, the twenty-seven young boys that made up the squad of the Martins Ferry football team could barely contain their excitement. Not only were they preparing for an unprecedented trip hundreds of miles away from their home, but perhaps more exciting, they were not required to attend school that day.

The team met downtown and traveled south several miles to Bridgeport via streetcar along the road now known as Ohio State Route 7, also known as the Ohio Scenic Byway. Bridgeport was the location for the bridge spanning the Ohio River, crossing Wheeling Island, and connecting to Wheeling proper on the eastern shore. Unfortunately, because the line intended to carry them across was malfunctioning that day, many of the boys ended up walking across the bridge on foot to board another streetcar that would take them to the Wheeling train station.

Shortly before 9:00 a.m., they boarded the special Pullman car Mullaney had helped obtain for the journey. The large car separated into as many as six separate compartments that converted into areas for seating or sleeping, with two lavatories on each end. Each car also was manned by an African American porter to cater to the boys' and chaperones' needs. Upon boarding, boys being boys, they wasted no time in taking advantage of the luxurious accommodations, obnoxiously ordering the porter around while claiming doe-eyed ignorance of the practice of "tipping" the help.

Come 11:30 the train had traveled as far as Pittsburgh. Upon arrival, the boys disembarked for a short lunch trip into the city. Their eyes immediately fixed on the ornate stonework and arches of the station and the looming buildings across the street and beyond. Many were astonished to get their first glimpse of actual skyscrapers, and they were quickly identified as "hayseeds" as they walked forward while peering skyward, trying to count the number of floors in the buildings above. Given only two short hours in the city, they grabbed their meal as quickly as possible to maximize sightseeing before returning to the Pullman and continuing on to Harrisburg.

They arrived at their destination at around 7:00 p.m. and, like any group of high school kids sleeping in close quarters, had difficulty settling down to sleep. The Pullman, which served as their lodging on this trip, was able to convert into upper- and lower-deck sleeping arrangements. Despite the swanky accommodations, there was nothing to be done about the noise—laughter often being led by Cyril himself playing cards with a small group—or the loud snoring coming from Frank Bowen, the Martins Ferry athletic director. Bowen at one point fell from the upper deck to the floor of the car, which apparently was a disruptive enough occasion that everyone finally began to settle down for the evening.

The next morning, Owens kept the team close, stressing upon them the need to rest before the evening's big game. At mid-morning, he led the team to a field outside the city limits— an area where the State Militia kept its horses—and led a brief practice before returning to the Pullman for more rest. The big game was nearly upon them.

At the appointed time, the team made the trek to Harrisburg Tech high school. In an emotional meeting with the team, coach, and chaperones present, they discussed the importance of the game, its historic nature for the Martins Ferry program, and the potential to showcase their hometown talents to the to the scouts in the stadium that had come to witness the game. There was an opportunity before them for the taking.

Bud Mullaney then took Cyril aside to impress upon him individually the importance of the day's game. He looked his young protégé in the eye and asked him to "show me (this) day the best brand of football you ever put out." Cyril replied with deep seriousness, muttering only two words: "I will."

Shortly before 2:30 in the afternoon, the Ferrians took the field.

HARRISBURG TECH WAS a nationally recognized high school football team, and it did not take long to figure out why. As the home team took the field, it was clear that they operated at a level Ferry hadn't yet seen. The first thing noticed was their size. Each Harrisburg player outweighed the Ferry team by at least 20 pounds per man. According to the *Harrisburg Register*, the "preponderance of gross tonnage" was impossible to ignore, and it was a distinct and significant advantage.

Nevertheless, Ferry took the field with confidence and hope, knowing that this year Harrisburg's team had, unbelievably, lost three straight games, all by close margins— something previously unheard of in the history of their program. So while Ferry saw the potential to take on an exemplary program in a down year, Harrisburg saw the game as a "must-win" to get back on track.

As captain, Cyril won the coin toss and elected to defend the north goal, meaning they would receive the kickoff at the beginning of the second half. The teams took the field, and Letzelter kicked off. Harrisburg returned his deep kick to their 23-yard line, where the contest began.

On the Harrisburg roster was a young, emerging star by the name of Johnny Kitzmiller, who came to be known as the "Flying Dutchman." Only a sophomore for this matchup, he was nonetheless an extraordinarily talented player who would eventually go on to play at Oregon and become one of the first great stars for the Oregon Ducks.

At this point, however, he was still an unknown. And unbeknownst to Ferry, he was about to have a breakout game.

During the first drive, Kitzmiller shared ball-carrying duties, gaining ground at about 3 yards per try. The Tech machine was slowly eating up the field, only to be regularly pushed backward by their own penalties. They eventually lost the ball on downs at midfield.

As Ferry took the field at the 50, the Harrisburg crowd watched as Cyril gained 20 yards in three plays and delivered his team to the Tech 30-yard line. At this point, the Tech defense keyed in on Letzelter, stopping his progress, and holding Ferry on downs.

After Tech's Kitzmiller got things going with a quick 5-yard gain and a teammate added another 18, on their third play of the possession, they coughed up the ball just inside Ferry territory.

After two attempts to run the ball had gained no yardage, Cyril dropped back for a pass that was intercepted deep in Tech territory. After two short gains, Tech elected to punt out of danger, and Ferry took possession once again at midfield.

Cyril quickly completed a 23-yard pass to Wells, getting the ball to the Tech 25-yard line. Ferry then attempted a triple-pass play that took Letzelter for a 5-yard loss. They quickly regained the yards on a quick run through the right guard before the whistle ended the first quarter.

Starting the second quarter with a third and 10 from the Tech 25-yard line, Ferry attempted two consecutive forward passes, both of which were grounded. They once again gave up the ball on downs.

Tech now quickly responded with a series of punishing runs, including a 26-yard scamper that got Harrisburg to the Ferry 43-yard line. After a few short-yardage plays, Tech tossed the ball to Kitzmiller, who carried it around the right end for 35 yards and the team's first touchdown of the year. He then followed up with his own successful goal kick, and Harrisburg had the lead, 7-0.

Ferry took possession to no avail and quickly saw itself punting again. This time, Cyril kicked all the way to the Harrisburg 2-yard line, only to see the ball quickly returned to the 23. Harrisburg once again went to work, eating up the field in vast chunks. Within a handful of plays, they'd brought the ball back to midfield. But Ferry then held firm to force the punt.

As Tech fell back to punt, Ferry sophomore Jack Burd positioned himself to receive the kick. His attempt to catch the ball on his own 15 slipped through his hands, and Tech smothered the ball, regaining position deep in enemy territory.

Kitzmiller wasted no time in connecting with a forward pass that earned them a first and goal from the Ferry 5-yard line. He then carried the ball right through the center of the line for his second touchdown of the day. In just a few short minutes of game time, what had been a battle of trench warfare had turned into a commanding lead for Harrisburg.

And then, just as it seemed the second quarter could not get any worse, during the final minutes of the half, fellow Ferry senior and playmaker Clem Siandru was injured on an attempted forward pass and carried off the field.

As the half ended, Cyril hadn't made any mistakes and had shown he was clearly the engine of his team. But he had not yet "seized the opportunity" before him. Letzelter would enter the second half with more pressure and less help than initially anticipated. And he knew dozens of prominent eyes were watching that could determine his future.

Coming in for the second half, Letzelter was unquestionably fired up. His first opportunity to touch the ball was a punt reception that he accepted at his own 40-yard line, which he then exploded through the Tech special teams for a 30-yard return, setting his team up on the Tech 30-yard line.

After Ferry had attempted two unsuccessful runs and an incomplete pass, Jack Burd dropped back and flipped the ball 10 yards upfield to Letzelter. Cyril caught the ball and headed toward the Tech goal with single-minded purpose. As he crossed the Tech goal line, he was carrying two Harrisburg players on his back as he ran. Even the home-field fans took notice.

Ferry's defense then stiffened considerably. During the next possession, they held Harrisburg to downs and fielded their punt at their own 20-yard line. Cyril then executed a double-pass play, which, along with a Tech penalty, got the ball to the Ferry 45. Cyril then busted open another big run of 18 yards to get the ball once again deep into Tech territory.

After another short run and another Tech penalty, Ferry was lining up for a first down on the Harrisburg 30. After a quick attempt by Charles Griffith for no gain, they handed the ball for Letzelter again for 5 yards and then inexplicably did not call his number for either of the next two plays. Once again, instead of scoring, they turned the ball back over to Tech on downs.

Despite their good fortune, Tech was unable to move the ball and punted. This time, Burd handled the ball and ran it back to the opposing 43. However, two plays later, Burd threw an interception to Kitzmiller that he caught on his own 20 and ran back 55 yards to the Ferry 25, stopping the Ohio team's momentum in its tracks, and flipping the field to boot. Kitzmiller's spectacular play brought the third period to a close.

As the fourth quarter began, a series of plays, including 12 total yards for Kitzmiller, brought Tech to fourth and goal. Rather than kick for the easy three points, they went for it, and Ferry held. However, even though they held, their situation was precarious. After two unsuccessful attempts to advance the ball, Ferry quickly punted, and Kitzmiller received the ball and ran it back to the Ferry 28. A series of short runs moved the ball to the 7-yard line, at which point Kitzmiller drop-kicked for another 3 points, effectively putting the game out of reach.

Nevertheless, Ferry took what would obviously be the last possession of the contest and tried to make the most of it. On the first play, Cyril broke for an 11-yard run around the left end, only to be called back on a penalty. Letz then threw a 16-yard pass to get to the 36-yard line. A 10-yard pass by Burd got them to the 45 with the seconds ticking off the clock. After two quick incomplete passes, Letzelter dropped back, spotted the injured Siandru who had reentered the game, and made a 20-

yard connection, getting Ferry to the Tech 35. At that point the game ended with Ferry defeated 17-7.

Without a doubt, the loss was a disappointment. Of greater concern to both Cyril and Mullaney was the perception of Letzelter's play. While he had unmistakably carried his team, the results still spoke for themselves. A loss is a loss.

However, the papers the next day in Harrisburg raved about Cyril's performance. While local hero Kitzmiller was clearly the star, locals pointed with wonder at the smaller fullback who carried two tacklers on his back as he scored and noted his ability to run, kick, punt, and pass. According to the *Harrisburg Register*: "The team from the Ohio Valley trotted out a remarkable back in Letzelter, their captain, who turned in a most brilliant performance. Glenn Killinger, the old Penn State star who witnessed the game, pronounced him one of the most promising youngsters he had ever seen, and stated that he would have Hugo Bezdek get after him for Penn State."

In short, while Ferry may have lost their first game of the season, the primary mission had been accomplished. Mullaney had provided a larger stage for Cyril to perform on front of an important audience, and he rose to the task. The recruitment of Cyril Letzelter was officially underway.

CYRIL STILL HAD his senior season to finish. The Harrisburg game had taken place at the midpoint of the schedule. Ferry's defeat at the hands of the team from central Pennsylvania was not only disappointing, but it also appeared to affect the team's play. Reports of the game against Shadyside, the Saturday after the team returned from Harrisburg and Washington, D.C., described a lackluster team effort that was overcome only by the individual play of both Letzelter and Siandru. Cyril, at times playing quarterback, had a solid day, with a 20-yard pass to Skip Moore to score the final touchdown in their 19-0 win.

The following week against Adena, the team appeared to have recovered its sharpness, as they routed their opponent 65-6. By all accounts, the team came together after halftime. Going in for the break, the Ferrians held a 19-6 lead. But upon taking the field in the third quarter, they exploded for 33 more points before the fourth quarter began. Cyril had another big game, setting up the first touchdown with a 9-yard run to the Adena 1, which Siandru quickly converted. Cyril also caught a short pass near the line of scrimmage and impressively turned it into a 35-yard reception for the team's third score.

Alternating between fullback and quarterback, Letzelter led his team to their third quarter eruption, passing for one touchdown and running 30 yards for another on the ground. Once it was clear that the rout was on, Coach Owens pulled his captain to save him for the next week's big game; the most important of the year, as always, against their archrival to the south: Bellaire.

BOTH TEAMS HAD spent the week before the game practicing in secret, utilizing the local police to hold a perimeter around their training fields to keep prying eyes away from the preparations for the big contest. These were considered the two fastest teams in the valley, and both had deep enough benches to ensure an intense game from the opening kickoff until the final whistle.

After occasionally experimenting in previous games with Cyril lining up for limited plays at the quarterback position, Coach Owens still surprised many by announcing before the game that Letzelter would, for the first time, be the team's starting quarterback. With Red Griffith, one of Ferry's big backfield boys, back and healthy after being sidelined with an injury, Owens felt the move would give his team a boost in size stacking up against the heavier Bellaire team. The decision made a certain amount of sense, but in so doing, Owens increased the pressure on his senior captain to carry them in the biggest game of the year, while primarily playing a position outside his comfort zone.

The excitement as the game grew near was palpable. Local news reports estimated that a crowd of at least 7,000 was expected to witness the contest at Martins Ferry's League Park, and the papers carried warnings from law enforcement authorities that wagering on the game was strictly banned. And yet, the media also carefully noted that "those who care to risk their greenbacks on their choice or sentiment are plying an active trade." The reports added that, while the early betting showed Bellaire to be favored 4 to 3, "before game time these (odds) should be lengthened, judging from the huge bank rolls being flourished around Bellaire, and the scarcity of actual purple cash in the up-the-river camp."

When, after much anticipation, Saturday afternoon finally arrived, the skies were gray and overcast and marked by a chilly November wind out of the north. The weather did not dampen the enthusiasm, however, as an estimated 10,000 to 12,000 spectators showed up for the game, exploding the previous estimates for attendance. The schools had anticipated large crowds and arranged for eleven additional sections of bleachers to be brought in by Bellaire, but it wasn't nearly enough. The assembled crowd was far too large to be accommodated by the bleachers and the room available outside of the fence encircling the field. Enough people had perched upon the barriers that they were buckling under the strain, and the police had to rope off the south end zone to keep the masses at bay. The standing-room-only crowd was several people deep.

The size of the crowd brought to mind the cliché suggesting that if ever there was a time to break the law in Martins Ferry, this was it. Not only was every single member of the Martins Ferry Police Department present and in uniform for crowd control, but Bellaire had brought four officers of their own to help patrol the visiting fans. It was, nevertheless, a raucous scene, featuring bedlam of all types, including a group of Ferry lads parading around the field before the game displaying a funeral wreath for Bellaire.

Pregame chatter billed the big competition, correctly, as a clash between the two best players in the valley—Cyril Letzelter vs. Bellaire's backfield star, Obie Miles. On the Friday before the game, the *Wheeling Times* predicted that Miles would put up the better game, noting, "With both Miles and Letzelter in form and a valley title hanging upon their work, these 2 all valley girders should furnish the fireworks of this four-round conflict. Of the two, we would pick Miles to shine more brilliantly as an individual as Letzelter, as team captain, has been sacrificing himself all year for the sake of teamwork and team play."

The spectators bore witness to one heck of a game. The *Wheeling Times* later called it "the Greatest Game in Valley History." Obviously, how one felt about the contest depended

106

heavily on one's perspective. Nevertheless, the *Times* accurately stated, "those who had the pleasure of being among those present were treated to a grid battle that spilled fight from goal to goal, sensational hard football in every department and a remarkable exhibition of the pastime by two equally matched high school elevens." It was a game that would be discussed years after the fact.

The game itself started just like any other, with the Martins Ferry High School Band, trimmed in purple and white, taking the field to play an hour before the starting whistle. A half hour later, when both teams took to the field for pregame warm-ups, the crowd was already standing room only, with hundreds still waiting to enter the confines. The *Bellaire Daily Leader* noted, "Virtually every living member of the Bellaire alumni were present."

Martins Ferry won the toss and elected to defend the north goal, fielded the opening kickoff at their own 20, and ran it to the 30 before being stopped. Cyril then went quickly to work, zipping around the left end on first down for five yards before being stopped by Miles. On second down, however, Homer Wells took the handoff from Letzelter and then promptly fumbled the ball, recovered it, and was then tackled for a big loss. Ferry elected to punt on third down, which set the visitors up to begin their offense at midfield.

Bellaire responded with a quick 5-yard run by Miles that was negated by a personal foul penalty against the visitors for piling on. Harold S. Williams, the Ferry center, was knocked out cold and carried from the field. After two plays that covered only 3 yards, Bellaire punted the ball back. Two plays later Ferry fumbled again, only this time they were not so lucky, as

Bellaire recovered. The error would prove costly. While both teams would trade possessions again, the visitors would eventually succeed in taking advantage of the very good field position, grinding out enough yardage to take the lead on a 1-yard run by Miles.

Nevertheless, the punishing, trench-warfare style of play continued, and so it went for most of the afternoon: inspired backbreaking play by both sides, occasionally interrupted by turnovers, penalties, and miscues, and very limited scoring.

Throughout the first half, most of Cyril's impact was uncharacteristically coming from his arm, and not all of it good. Despite some successful short passes, he gave up a critical interception to Miles midway through the second quarter—Ferry's third turnover of the game. On his next possession, however, Cyril went back to relying on his feet. With runs of 8, 6, and 4 yards, along with a well-executed triple-pass play, he led Ferry to the Bellaire 4-yard line. But Bellaire stiffened. A succession of four straight running plays, three by Cyril himself, netted only 2 yards, and Ferry saw a golden opportunity to score slip from their fingers.

The second half proceeded much as the first, with Coach Owens leaning on Cyril to produce offense via the forward pass, and the longer the game went on, the clearer it became that the game plan Owens had drawn up did not play to his captain's strengths. While many passes were successful, just as many fell incomplete; and in the fourth quarter alone, Cyril threw three interceptions, for a total of five on the day.

Ferry never scored, and the early fumble, along with Bellaire's late-second-quarter goal line stand, was enough for visitors to eke out the win.

Every game has a winner and a loser. And when two communities are so deeply invested in a contest, there is glory and blame to be assigned. This game was no different.

If one considers the thinking going into the match—that it would boil down to a battle between Letzelter and Miles—the tale of the tape tells a very unambiguous story. In nearly every aspect of the game, Cyril was the most impactful player on the field all day. He carried the ball 21 times, never losing yardage, and netting 68 yards. Miles, by comparison, carried the ball 18 times, netting only 16 yards.

And this says nothing of Cy's impact in the passing game. While Bellaire as a team only completed two passes on the day for a total of 33 yards, Letzelter himself completed eight passes for 82 yards. On the day, Cyril had personally accounted for 60 percent of Ferry's offense, while Miles had only accounted for 31 percent for Bellaire.

But these statistics don't tell the entire story. The fact was that Cyril, coached into executing a pass-heavy game plan, threw five interceptions. And when he had his chance to shine late in the second quarter to tie the game, he fell short. He also missed a field goal attempt.

And so, despite the tale of the tape, Obie Miles was able to claim the winning touchdown as a result of 1 of the 16 yards he gained on the ground and was, therefore, the "hero." Uncharacteristically, Cyril Letzelter found himself in the unfamiliar position of being the "goat."

Years later, local sportswriter Don Hamill revisited the famous game in a column for the *Wheeling Daily News*, providing new insights never before shared about how Bellaire had stopped Letzelter.

Hamill focused on the noteworthy drive where Cyril was uncharacteristically unable to burst through for the short yardage needed to tie the game. He had an interesting story to tell. According to Hamill, while it was Obie Miles who had been in the position to tackle Letzelter on every play in that four-play series, the real hero had been Bellaire's center, Tony Matusek. Hamill explained, "As centers go, (Matusek) was the outstanding pivot man in the valley, despite his small size. Tony's greatness came from a fighting heart, and an uncanny ability to remember figures and plays."

Matusek, apparently, had a freakish ability to remember call signals and plays after experiencing them on the field just one time. After the first quarter, for the rest of the game, Matusek had seen enough to enable him to set the Bellaire defense so that they were in an optimal position to stop the Ferry eleven.

On the fateful drive, as Cyril called the signals for Ferry, Matusek would "turn and give instruction to Miles. The play started, and Miles made the tackles which prevented a touchdown. Four times he did this."

Matusek's capacity to remember Ferry's signals was not only pivotal in that crucial defensive stand, but also in the uncharacteristic number of turnovers Ferry made during that game. Beyond Letzelter's five interceptions, the team also coughed up at least three fumbles.

Regardless of how they won the game, the Bellaire contest in 1924 would be long remembered by player and fan alike. And there are indications that the outcome rattled Cyril as the season moved toward its end.

AS A PERSON who was both of Catholic and German descent, Cyril was an easy target for abuse during this highly charged and bigoted era, regardless of his exploits on the gridiron. And if ever there was a plausible moment for such nastiness to reach its peak during his senior year, it was after the game against Bellaire.

Mullaney's correspondence with Cyril at his graduation made it clear that he came in for abuse that year at some point from "bigots and fools who have made the road doubly hard for you." However, it was not in the young boy's nature to complain. In fact, he had a reputation as an easygoing, quick-to-smile teenager. And while there is little evidence remaining that clearly identifies what form this abuse took, one can make some educated guesses.

The rest of the season after the Bellaire game was noteworthy only insofar as Ferry unquestionably lost whatever spring had been their step. The next week they were shut out at home for a rare loss against Buchannon, and the following week they traveled to Linsly, where they managed a 0-0 tie on a field that was ankle deep in mud. Heading into the final game against Bridgeport, it had been almost a month since the Ferry offense scored.

In a community "crazy" for football, it isn't hard to envision local fans growing jaded by the team's slump and directing at least some of their frustration at the team captain and undisputed offensive leader. Two unique keepsakes found within Cyril Letzelter's voluminous scrapbooks detailing his football years support this conclusion. Buried within pages upon pages of local articles describing his 1922–24 seasons at Martins Ferry sat one small news story, pasted near another article detailing the disappointing 1924 loss to Bellaire.

The piece begins by describing a verbal, postseason altercation that Ferry coach Yip Owens had on a public street with two local men regarding charges the men made that the 1924 team had a "yellow streak" and charges that "one student in particular" was a "quitter." And while the story details Owens's vigorous defense of his team and of the unnamed player, the piece quickly shifts to a tone of admonition to the community as a whole for spreading gossip that "spreads rapidly and sometimes does serious injury."

No notes or markings of any kind appear on this particular clipping. However, its distinct placement in the scrapbook, combined with Letzelter's role as team captain and consensus best player, makes it likely that he was, in fact, the unnamed player mentioned in the article.

Another item that supports this theory is the local story about the postseason banquet hosted by the local booster club. The season had fortunately finished on a high note, with a 20-14 win over Bridgeport where Cyril had rebounded with a stellar performance and accounted for all three touchdowns in the win. Despite the mid-season slump, his team had finished with a respectable 7-3-1 record, and as in previous years, the boosters wanted to celebrate the seniors, award varsity letters, and announce the election of the football captain for the next year.

The banquet featured music by the high school orchestra and speeches by the school superintendent, members of the Board of Education, and Principal Beman Ludwig (who would later become Cyril's brother-in-law). Mullaney received plaudits for his role in setting up the contest in Harrisburg, and the community received warm praise for its ongoing support for the program.

However, when it came time for the seniors to speak, news reports noted with surprise that "Captain Letzelter had quietly disappeared." Fellow teammate James Blackford was asked to speak in his place. For a person who had been a natural leader in so many ways already, and whose later career would reaffirm these attributes, it is a moment that sticks out as odd and very out-of-character.

The Bellaire game, the late-season slump, the vocal discontent in the community, and Mullaney's words of praise for how Cyril held up in the face of abuse from "bigots and fools" all point to a rocky conclusion to Cyril's high school football career.

And as if he wasn't carrying enough on his shoulders, Cyril was faced with a decision no one else in his family had ever faced: Would he continue to play football and go to college? Could he handle college? And if so, how could it be afforded? Where would he go?

Fortunately for Cyril, he had his patron and guardian angel, John Francis Mullaney, to help lead him to the next stage of his life.

Proselytizing

As his senior season progressed, there was little doubt that Cyril would have the opportunity to be the first of his family to attend college. In the weeks and months after the Harrisburg game, with Mullaney's help, he would be courted by schools like Penn State, Columbia, Yale, and Carnegie Tech—just to name a few.

However, as the courtship of young Letzelter was getting underway, the collegiate community and the nation were already in the midst of a furious debate over the practice of "proselytizing" by academic institutions—or as we call it today, "recruiting."

Unlike the modern era, where nearly all controversy revolves around the possibility and manner of students receiving financial gain while playing in the collegiate ranks, in the 1920s it was the very idea of luring top talent to an institution of higher learning based on their athletic skill that was controversial. At this point in the decade, the debate had yet to really mature into a discussion of individual issues such as scholarships, ghost employment, cash payments, and beyond.

The movement for reform of collegiate football had accelerated as the sport exploded during the first half of the decade. The end of the Great War was a significant driver of the explosion in popularity, to be sure. But perhaps as important was the fact that the sport did not just return to a prewar status quo; it actually expanded in both reach and quality. The sport was no longer dominated by the Big Three, Big Ten, and the leading schools on the West Coast. Each season saw the emergence of more quality programs, driven in part by the popularity of the sport at the high school level.

It is impossible to know which came first: the thirst for lower-profile schools to cash in on the booming popularity of football or the awareness of the deep reservoir of talent being developed in working-class communities across the nation. Regardless, in retrospect, it quickly became plain that talent for the sport wasn't confined to the class of undergraduates that pointed toward the Ivy League or other major schools.

As the industrialization of America and the growth of the economy in the 1920s continued to explode, it brought with it an increasing need for a better-educated, middle-class workforce. This need produced new opportunities for working-class boys to access a level of education unavailable to previous generations. At the same time, more and more colleges saw the chance to lure many of these boys to their schools to run highly profitable football programs.

The expanding popularity of the sport led to its next obvious problem: lack of stadium capacity to meet growing demand. With astonishing quickness, many schools moved to build large stadiums to host their teams and reap the financial windfall. As Raymond Schmidt reported in his important work *Shaping College Football*, "Perhaps the most defining and long-lasting legacy of 1920s college football was the conversion of the sport into an unquestioned big-business venture for the schools as a by-product of the wave of stadium building that swept across the universities during the decade."

The thirst for larger venues was owed in part to the afterglow of the war, which had infused the population with a heartfelt sense of national pride. Battles on the gridiron seemed a way for the public to recapture the excitement of victory after a hard-fought battle. Some writers of the era actually viewed football as a necessary part of the "cooling off" process for the country after the war. In fact, in many cases, the athletic officials pushing for larger venues used an appeal to patriotism to win approval for their plans. Many stadium plans from the era included special memorials for those lost in the war, and more than a few new stadiums themselves were christened "Memorial Stadium," including those erected at Illinois and California.

In a sense, the building of a stadium was a point of no return for a school. Such massive structures required revenue sources to be sustained, which meant the seats needed to be filled, which required that the product on the field be of sufficient quality to attract fans. And so, whether or not a school had previously been engaged in proselytizing, once the concrete began to pour, they really had little choice.

ALTHOUGH THE WIDESPREAD popularity of football was growing by the day, there were still significant populations that were greatly concerned about the growing commercialism of the sport and how it was detracting from the academic mission of the schools. Led primarily by professors and educational administrators, they fought vainly to return football to the minor place it held before the turn of the century. Nothing worried them more than the growing sense that their rightly prized educational institutions were increasingly being recognized for their prowess on the gridiron as opposed to the success of their graduates.

Their efforts were nothing new. The arguments they espoused dated back more than two decades, decrying the growing dependence of schools on football revenue, the act of recruiting, and what they saw as the influence of alumni in steering focus away from the classrooms toward the playing field. However, the explosion of interest in the 1920s only moved them to redouble their efforts, especially after having seen such promise for de-emphasis during the war years.

In 1924, as Cyril was playing his senior season, the newly named (and first) commissioner of the Western Conference, Major John Griffith, was already working to discourage the efforts of overzealous alumni in recruiting players to conference schools. Griffith, when appointed in 1922, had been surprised to find that the "interpretation" of one of the conference regulations "practically says that it is desirable for alumni to recruit athletic material from high schools." Griffith quickly set out to change that perception and interpretation.

A 1924 memo to the league's athletic directors went so far as to cite occasions where conference rules had been broken regarding the influence of outside groups and suggested that each athletic director relay letters to alumni explaining the official opposition to recruitment. The following year, seeing very limited improvement, Griffith himself penned a letter to every high school principal in areas represented by Western Conference schools explaining the prohibitions on recruiting and asking for their help in reporting abuse.

A real turning point for the reformers came in October 1925. The president of Franklin & Marshall College, Dr. Henry H. Apple, penned an article that detailed a wide array of abuses in the sport and decried the attention and emphasis the game was taking from the educational mission of higher education. However, what set Apple's article apart from others that came before was his explicit suggestion that an investigation of the sport should be commissioned, saying that such an investigation "might establish that some universities deliberately and officially offer scholarships and other inducements as a reward for athletic ability, especially football."

Within weeks, the heads of fifteen other colleges had signed a letter supporting Apple's idea, although notably none from the largest football schools. Nevertheless, the idea of a nationwide investigation quickly gained steam. At one point, a consensus began to form around the creation of five separate educational committees to conduct the inquiry. However, almost as quickly the reformers began to realize that a study controlled by academia would have no more credibility in addressing the problem than a study guided by athletic directors and coaches. What was needed was an independent body with the credibility to lead an investigation.

It was this recognition that led several college heads to submit a proposal to the Carnegie Foundation for the Advancement of Teaching. The foundation, which was initiated by Andrew Carnegie in 1905 and then chartered by an act of Congress in 1906, was "committed to developing networks of ideas, individuals, and institutions to advance teaching and learning." In January 1926, the foundation accepted the challenge from the college heads and provided the resources for a project director and five full-time researchers. The project quickly got to work. It would take three years to complete, but the scope and detail of the final report resulted in the most comprehensive analysis of the relationship between football and academia to date.

When the Carnegie Report was finally released, the *New York Times* trumpeted the findings in an explosive, page-one story on Thursday, October 24, 1929. Headlined "College Sports Tainted by Bounties, Carnegie Fund Finds in Wide Study," the write-up not only had coveted front-page space, but it also took up nearly all news space on pages 22 and 23 of that morning's addition. The Carnegie team had looked deep into the programs of 130 different collegiate football programs and found all but twenty-eight failed to run "clean" programs. Of the twenty-eight clean programs, only eight were considered to be major football schools.

The Carnegie investigators laid out in exhaustive detail the four main ways in which programs subsidized their athletes. Those included providing loans, providing jobs that may or may not require significant actual work, providing scholarships, and providing "miscellaneous assistance"—a reference to the practice of many schools to use "slush funds" to compensate specifically recruited athletes.

The report, lamenting that the "self-respecting American undergraduate does not solicit charity," decried loans that were often directed by local businessmen, alumni, or fraternal organizations, and, more often than not, arranged by the individual who recruited the athlete. It detailed jobs provided in which "there is a vast difference between honest work for which fair wages are received and the 'sinecures' often reserved for athletes (and) paid out of all proportion to the value of services rendered." A wide array of scholarship programs had been designed based wholly or in part on an athlete's value to the organization. Additionally, such programs were distributed unevenly when compared from school to school. For example, the Pennsylvania State College and New York University granted as many as seventy-five scholarships, while other schools offered twenty-five scholarships or fewer.

The most blatant form of subsidization, however, came in the form of cold, hard cash. Sometimes offered to defer college expenses, and sometimes offered as a reward for an already-subsidized athlete who helped recruit additional talent, these "black box" programs could exist both inside or independent of the athletic program. As a rule, however, these funds were dispersed based on the needs of the recruit, with the recruiter often authorized to offer anything up to the total cost of tuition, board, and room. In some cases, additional funds were disbursed to top performers as "paychecks." Schools or alumni associations would maintain funds capable of distributing between $25,000 and $50,000 per year—the modern-day equivalent of $300,000 to $600,000.

Looking back at the report with the benefit of over eight decades of hindsight, what stands out is that the investigators received a level of cooperation from the schools in compiling information that seems unthinkable today, and that the schools surely regretted in retrospect. Nearly one-third of the *New York Times* story on the report was a series of responses from academic and athletic leaders from fourteen major programs— all either expressing surprise, doubt, or outright denial of the report's findings.

The media coverage was clearly written with the expectation that the conclusions would shake the foundations of the world of academic sport. And for a short time, perhaps it did; the initial response of the colleges certainly suggests they were bracing for a backlash. However, the *Times* story hit near the end of the week, in the Thursday papers. On national news stories, most regional outlets relied on the *Times* or other news wire services, so many got their first exposure to the story on Friday and headed into the weekend.

As people returned to work the following Monday, the stock market crashed, with the Dow Jones Industrial Average dropping 38.33 points. The next day, known forever as "Black Tuesday," the Dow dropped another 30 points. In just two short days, nearly 25 percent of the nation's wealth invested in the stock market simply vanished.

The Great Depression had begun, and the Carnegie Report was quickly forgotten.

BACK IN 1924, however, the Carnegie Report had yet to be commissioned. Therefore, Cyril was wrapping up his senior season in the same college football recruiting environment that the report would later describe and denounce five years in the future. However, the report serves as a useful prism through which to look back upon the complicated dance between prospect and school that Mullaney conducted on his protégé's behalf over the following six months.

Mullaney, having already arranged and executed the trip to Harrisburg that provided a high-profile public showcase for Cyril's football talents, now turned his focus toward leveraging his relationships on Letzelter's behalf. As he had time and again before, Mullaney tapped into his broad network of Roman Catholic allies throughout the region. In this case, none was more important that John F. LaBoon of Pittsburgh.

Locally, LaBoon was best known as the longtime director of Public Works of Allegheny County, who at one point played a pivotal role working with Pittsburgh mayor David L. Lawrence to get all other county municipalities on board for the creation of the Allegheny County Sanitary District. Local sports fans, however, knew him for his long and active involvement in athletic programs at Carnegie Tech, where he once played as an undergraduate and now served on the University Board of Trustees and the Carnegie Tech Athletic Council.

The Carnegie Institute of Technology, as it was formally known, was founded in 1900 by the famous Pittsburgh philanthropist Andrew Carnegie. His original vision was to create a series of technical schools aimed at providing vocational education for the children of the working class. For its first twelve years, the new and growing institution was only known as the Carnegie Technical Schools. It was only after the school began issuing four-year degrees in 1912 that it formally adopted the "Institute of Technology" moniker.

The Carnegie Schools first started playing organized football in 1906, notching seven different coaches in their first seven years as an active program. The program's beginnings were less than impressive, with only 21 wins during this period, compared to 40 losses. During this time, the Carnegie teams were generally known as the Skibos—a reference to the name of Andrew Carnegie's ancient castle and residence in the Scottish Highlands. While later teams dropped the Skibo moniker, their current nickname of the Tartans remains a nod to the founder's Scottish connection.

Tech's football fortunes didn't really begin to turn until the arrival of Walter P. Steffen as head coach. Upon his addition, the team and program slowly began to improve. He posted his first winning record in 1915 and repeated the trick the following season. However, it was not until 1920—after seven years on the job—that Steffen was able to produce a win over what was considered a major opponent: Washington & Jefferson, whom they beat 6-0.

In 1922, Coach Knute Rockne of Notre Dame added Carnegie to its list of opponents for a simple reason. The Skibos were of a class of football programs that major schools could schedule for a reliable "down week," allowing the major team to fill their schedule with a low-stress game yet still be an overwhelming favorite for the win. This was a common scheduling tactic that continues to the modern day.

In 1924, Notre Dame was traveling to Pittsburgh to meet the Skibos on their home turf. Grantland Rice had already written his glowing prose baptizing the Notre Dame backfield as the "Four Horsemen" in November of that year. Most people knew, then, that Rockne's team appeared the most dominant in the nation and only had one stop left in Pittsburgh before a meeting against Stanford in the Rose Bowl on New Year's Day that would crown the National Champion.

Mullaney undoubtedly knew that the draw of the Catholics to Pittsburgh would be a potential recruiting bonanza, with the contest drawing scores of coaches and hundreds of potential recruits. He was not wrong. News reports estimated that at least 20 major program coaches planned to attend the game.

Cyril would be in attendance as well, with a bit of an advantage. Relying on the help of his friend John LaBoon, Mullaney secured sideline passes for himself and Cyril. As a result, Letzelter was one of only two high school prospects given the privilege of watching the game from the Carnegie Tech sideline that Saturday, while the hundreds of other hopefuls watched from the stands of Forbes Field.

The fact that Cyril was a special guest of LaBoon was a distinct tip of the hand regarding where he (and Mullaney) were targeting their efforts for the future. But that did not prevent them both from taking full advantage of the occasion. In fact, as the Wheeling *Intelligencer* reported: "During the day, Letzelter and Mullaney met some of the big coaches in the country, including Stagg of Chicago, Bezdek of Penn State, Wilce of Ohio State, Spears of West Virginia, Zuppke of Illinois, Young of University of Pennsylvania, and Kerr, former Pittsburgh boy now assistant coach (to Glenn 'Pop' Warner) at Leland Stanford University."

Despite the interest from schools across the nation, the local news coverage focused primarily on Cyril's interaction with Coach Steffen and his assistants, with whom he met both before and after the game. Mullaney gave a detailed account to the *Wheeling Daily Times*:

> *Cyril Letzelter, Ferry High's grid captain this season, may enter Carnegie Tech next fall, as a result of the Ferry youngster's conference with Coach Steffen of Tech prior to Saturday's game with Notre Dame. Letz had a long talk with*

124

Carnegie authorities, both before and after the game, and while no definite promises were given it is understood he was impressed with the Pittsburgh school and the opportunities afforded.

Steffen sized up Letz carefully but was fooled about his weight. J. F. Mullaney asked Steffen to guess at his weight, and the latter hazarded an estimate of 155 pounds. Letz was taken into the gymnasium and tipped the beam at 179 pounds in his street clothes. After that, the Tartan mentor opened his eyes.

Letzelter was advised to report at Tech immediately after Ferry High closes next spring to take the entrance examination. If shy in any subjects he will be able to make up work by fall. Letz, who intends to take an engineering course, was advised that good school work will be a prime requisite for participation in Tech football.

While the immediate coverage firmly pointed to Carnegie Tech, and in some cases even announced that Letzelter had made a formal decision to attend Tech, he, in fact, remained open to the courting of other schools. In one case, it was reported that two representatives of West Virginia met with Cyril to induce him to enter that school. While local newspapers made it clear Cyril had not yet made a final decision, "it (was) understood a very tempting offer was made for his services by the West Virginia School."

In yet another case, Cyril met with officials from Penn State—a meeting so positive that some papers incorrectly reported that Letz had changed his mind and would be headed to Happy Valley instead.

Little evidence remains of how and when Cyril made his final decision to attend Carnegie Tech. Most likely, Cyril was always leaning strongly in that direction because of the influence and assistance of his mentor Mullaney. Also, given what was later revealed in the 1929 Carnegie Report, Tech reportedly operated one of the largest "slush funds" of any of the programs the study investigated—which offered a path for the comparatively poor Letzelter to be able to afford to attend the school. Given the previous interest conferred by such a wide variety of teams and the sponsorship of Mr. LaBoon, one has to assume that either the school or alumni had picked up the costs of Cyril's tuition, room, and board.

However, the most definite and verifiable assistance Cyril received came from Mullaney himself. Immediately after graduating from Ferry High, he quickly used his influence as the Superintendent of the nearby Yorkville Tin Plant to provide him an additional source of income to supplement whatever assistance he would be receiving from Carnegie Tech. For the rest of his college career, every summer, a well-paying, highly coveted job would be waiting for Cyril in Yorkville to ensure he had extra money in his pocket as he went through school.

To be sure, this was no "ghost" job. Mullaney, who believed in both the value of an education and the idea of a fair wage for honest work, assigned Cyril to the most punishing job in the Yorkville Tin Plant: that of the "bar catcher."

To understand the context of this position, one must recognize that a tin plant housed a distinct type of mill dedicated to taking "tin plate bars," which would have been

126

forged at a different location, and drawing them out to a specified thickness. Ordinarily a tin mill would take these bars—usually about two feet long, seven inches wide, and between one-quarter and one-half inch thick—and run them repeatedly through a heating and rolling process, resulting in a multilayered sheet of tin as much as five feet long and two feet wide.

The tin mill machinery itself consisted of several parts. The first were a series of large cast-iron rollers, each machine with two rollers apiece, one atop the other. The top roll was adjustable, while the bottom roll was stationary. With adjustments to the uppermost roller, an incredible amount of downward force could be applied to the tin-plate bars.

The second part of the tin mill were the furnaces—generally two furnaces for each roller. The bars would be "charged" in the furnace until malleable enough to run through the rollers, where they would be systematically thinned and expanded. Generally speaking, at least two tin plate bars would be used to fashion a fully layered, properly sized tin plate.

The process required three workers to conduct. First came the "heater," who was responsible for charging the bars in the furnace. The second was the "roller," who fed the heated bars between the two massive cylindrical rollers. Finally came the "catcher," who handled the plate as it came out the other end of the rollers and then lifted the plate back over the mill (which was at least eight feet high) back to the "heater" so the process could be completed.

Every job at the plant, due to their physical nature and the incredible heat in which the jobs had to be performed, was punishing. But the "catcher" was considered by consensus to be the most punishing role, as it required not only the handling and lifting of dense and scorching steel but the repeated lifting of the unfinished product overhead back to the "heater." At least eight runs through the roller were necessary to complete one tin plate.

Cyril was placed in this role in part because of his youth. But it is also plain that Mullaney put him in this position to help him build his body and adapt to playing football at the next level.

BY THE END of the summer, Cyril removed all doubt by announcing his official intent to enroll at Carnegie Tech in the weeks ahead. While he may have known his plans well before, he and Mullaney waited until the last minute to make it official. The day before he was scheduled to report, the news broke in the *Wheeling News*, which stated, "After a summer's work catching on the bar shears in a tinplate mill, Cyril J. Letzelter, one of the best football players Martins Ferry High ever developed, is in fine condition for fall football practice at Carnegie Tech, Pittsburgh. 'Letz' will enter that institution next month."

In fact, he planned to report the very next day, as he had already received word to report to James Anderson, the freshman coach for Tech, on August 30. The next stage of Cyril's career was about to begin.

The Yearling

As Cyril set off for his new home on the campus of Carnegie Institute of Technology in August of 1925, it had been less than a year since he and his Martins Ferry teammates made their brief stop in Pittsburgh. Where previously he and his friends stood in collective awe viewing the city's size and its skyscrapers, Cyril now returned slightly older and certainly wiser to the ways of the world after months as the subject of intense recruitment by some of the most powerful college football programs in the East.

Carnegie Tech was like many colleges of the era in that it adhered to what was known as the "the three-year eligibility" rule, limiting students to only three years of varsity play on the football team. In real terms, this meant that that Cy's exploits on the football field were confined to the "plebe" team while he and the other freshmen focused primarily on their studies.

As the former star player back home in Ferry, Cyril was in for serious adjustment. New students on the Carnegie Tech campus regularly were referred to as "plebes" or "yearlings," which came with certain requirements and expectations. In fact, according to the Carnegie yearbooks of the period, the freshmen were required to identify themselves by wearing distinguishable red armbands and ensuring that their daily wardrobe included neckties bound in a distinct Windsor knot. According to "plebe regulations," all yearlings were required to move about campus with heads bowed and to exhibit customary meekness to the upperclassmen. Bowing to such submissive requirements could not have been easy for the

129

confident and outgoing Letzelter. In fact, it was despised by the class as a whole, as memorialized in that year's annual:

> *Sophomore's domination held us fast in its embrace, and branded were we with its emblems of tyranny — the ungodly stocking and the ever dangling arm-band . . . Trials followed, with disastrous results, and the plebeian cry for revenge rang throughout the avenues.*

Nonetheless, the yearling regulations do not seem to have stood in the way of a good time. Cyril's scrapbook from the era includes pages of autographs and notes from his classmates that paint a picture of a freshman year filled with activities and allusions to hijinks, leaving no doubt that "Letz" and his buddies were regularly defying the recent amendment to the United States Constitution that prohibited the consumption of alcohol.

In fact, according to family members, his aunt Laura Caton often spoke of the weekend trips Cyril made back to Martins Ferry with a group of Carnegie pals in tow. With his father and aunt Laura living across the street from one another, it was not uncommon for Cyril and his friends to set up camp at the Catons' for long games of cards and beer. Part of the reason for selecting the Catons' home was because it was in the Catons' basement that Mike Letzelter and John Caton used to make their own covertly and illegally home bottled beer. They nurtured their hidden alcohol until the occasion when a large batch of the pressurized bottles began exploding under pressure, creating a ruckus not unlike machine gun fire, only with the added benefit of the sour beer smell that descended upon their little German neighborhood.

In any event, being college boys, they certainly wanted to choose the location closest to the beer.

Laura Caton remembered this vividly and often shared the story of how Cyril and his pals entertained each other by feeding beer to the Caton family terrier, Mitzi. Years later, Laura often lamented that Cyril's hijinks had turned the unfortunate dog into an alcoholic, as for years after, she was unable to open her refrigerator without Mitzi whining for beer.

Despite the fact that he hailed from a financially modest family, it is noteworthy that during this period, Cyril managed to obtain ownership of a car that he used to travel back and forth from Pittsburgh. It was an uncharacteristic luxury for someone of Letzelter's background and is probably circumstantial proof either that he was getting a degree of cash assistance from Carnegie alumni or that enough of his education and boarding expenses were being covered to allow him to splurge with his summer earnings gained from the tin plant.

Treasures from the era seem to confirm that Cyril, while always approachable and a little bit ornery, had achieved a certain level of cool at Tech. In fact, in one of the pictures in his sophomore yearbook—for the members of his engineering school—Cyril appears in the front row, black hair trimmed tight on the sides, but uncharacteristically long and tousled on top. He wears what resembles an expensive leather long coat over his required suit and Windsor tie, and he looks slightly annoyed as he alone in the picture is holding a cigarette between his right thumb and forefinger down at his side. A distinct aura radiated

suggesting his time was wasted taking pictures, and at a minimum, the man was eager to get back to his smoke. One thing abundantly clear was that the college experience was not putting a dent in the confidence he would
need to succeed in Pittsburgh.

NOT LONG AFTER his arrival, Cyril began to practice for the freshman football team. He probably already knew that one of the two alumni representatives on Tech's Athletic Council was none other than Mullaney's good friend John F. Laboon. Another close acquaintance of Mullaney's, Clarence "Buddy" Overend, served as the graduate manager of the team. From Mullaney's perspective, there was little doubt that his protégé Cyril would receive proper attention and care.

Cyril arrived on campus with what was probably the best freshman football class in the school's history. The squad would have as its anchor Howard Harpster, a future member of the College Football Hall of Fame. Harpster was a solid, all-around athlete with uncanny kicking abilities and a preternatural confidence when throwing the forward pass. The Hall of Fame credits Harpster for being one of the first quarterbacks of the era to execute a pass from his own end zone, a telling anecdote that spoke to his confidence on the gridiron.

During his freshman year, Cyril, like most men on campus, joined the fraternity system, pledging Phi Kappa—a fraternity founded at Brown University in 1884. He also set up residence in an indistinct, four-story, brick men's dormitory situated in the "Hill" section of campus—Scobell Hall. His placement there was not surprising. Scobell at the time was the dorm most known for its "school spirit," with a yearbook from the period stating, "It is Scobell who urges the Tartans on with their pertinent football signs." Signatures in Cyril's yearbooks supported this contention as they revealed not only Cyril's role in making those infamous signs, but also the fact that his freshman year roommate was Anthony Sweet—another teammate who would go on with Cyril to excel playing varsity ball for the Tartans.

Even with its sporting reputation, Scobell also had a reputation for carrying the highest overall grade point average on campus—a fact that one could interpret as either despite or because of its connection to varsity sports. There is some evidence to suspect the latter as, years later, when Cyril attended his first year at West Point, he had uncharacteristic difficulty with the required class work, especially considering that, by then, he already had earned his four-year engineering degree at Tech.

As the plebe season began that fall, they faced what many regarded as their hardest yearling schedule to date, with matchups against Pitt, Washington & Jefferson, Westinghouse, and others.

The season got off to a fast start against Slippery Rock, which saw the young Tartans rack up a decisive 34-6 victory on the strength of two Letzelter touchdowns and a series of lengthy runs from scrimmage. In the 31-0 drubbing the Tartan Freshmen placed on Westinghouse, Cyril scored one touchdown and began to secure his role as the favored back in short yardage situations.

In a 7-0 win over the fearsome team from Washington & Jefferson College, Letzelter was the clear hero of the game even though he did not score. Instead, it was his electrifying kickoff return in incredibly muddy conditions all the way to the opposing 1-yard line that set up the winning score. Contemporary news reports indicated that, had it not been for the poor state of the field, Cyril would have scored easily.

The upcoming, fierce contest against the in-city rival, the University of Pittsburgh, gave the yearlings no time to savor their victory. In a game cut short in the middle of the third period to make way for planned dedication exercises for the new stadium, Cyril had another chance to be the hero but just missed scoring on a dropkick that would have broken the tie just before the game ended. The resulting 6-6 final score in the shortened game left both teams wondering what might have been.

For the Tartans it ended up being the only blemish on their record. As the yearling season proceeded, news reports began to describe the Tartan freshmen as "the best Yearling team this side of the Alleghenies." Three more victories made way for a critical final game against California Normal, which at the time had been making its own history defeating some of the strongest freshman teams in the country.

In that spectacular contest, the Carnegie yearlings came through with a narrow, 7-6 victory that was secured by Cyril's critical PAT after a touchdown by teammate Chester Limric. In so doing, the team became lauded as the very first unbeaten team in the history of Carnegie football. Their expected inclusion on the following year's varsity squad raised hopes that Carnegie Tech might someday be able to match up with the major programs in the East. Cyril, in particular, was being singled out for special acclaim:

Carnegie Tech's age-old dream of a fullback who can hit an opposing line with sufficient power to gain five yards seems about to be realized. Coach Steffen believes he has found the man of his dreams in C. Letzelter, the same youth who played fullback on the 1925 plebe team.

Letzelter weighs almost 180 pounds and is fast. He can start in a hurry and has driving power in abundance. . . . One of the most unusual merits of Letzelter is his ability to throw a forward pass with his left or his right hand. He heaves them with either hand with equal skill. His ability in this respect will likely give him the job of helping Harpster in throwing passes.

The presence of the highly skilled Howard Harpster in the backfield meant Cyril would rarely be called upon to execute a forward pass. Nevertheless, the underlying point remained: with Cyril, Harpster, and the rest of the freshmen set to join the varsity team the following year, there was a new sense of optimism among the fans of the Skibos. Waiting to shape them for battle on a bigger stage was their unique and driven head coach, Wally Steffen of Chicago, Illinois.

Varsity

Young Walter Steffen first came to the attention of the people of Chicago, and the nation, at the turn of the century. He was a high school phenom on the gridiron as the quarterback of his Chicago North Division team; Steffen led his eleven to an intersectional championship against a team of Brooklyn standouts. Not only did Steffen run up a 75-0 score on his opponents, but he also did it in less than three quarters, as the game was called early due to darkness.

When college came calling, Walter stayed close to home and attended the University of Chicago. Under the guidance of the legendary coach Amos Alonzo Stagg, Steffen began his sophomore year as a halfback while the star quarterback—and eventual legendary sportswriter—Walter Eckersall played his final season. The following year, Steffen stepped in as the quarterback and began a remarkable run of huge victories.

The 158-pound Steffen promptly made All-America each season and directed Chicago fortunes through some of the most crushing conquests ever leveled upon Midwestern powers. Illinois fell by scores of 63-0 and 42-6; Purdue was pounded 39-0, 56-0 and 39-0; Indiana crumbled to 33-8, 27-6 and 29-6 thrashings and Minnesota was victimized, 29-0. During Steffen's three varsity seasons, he scored 156 points and the Maroons were virtually unbeatable.

Stagg was unsparing in his praise, calling Steffen, "a devilishly clever, resourceful ball carrier," adding, "I have never seen anyone who could even approximate his abilities. He's shifty, and an artful dodger." Stagg's opinion of Steffen was so high, in fact, that he immediately offered him a spot on his coaching staff after his graduation in 1909.

While serving as Stagg's assistant, Steffen went on to obtain his law degree in 1912 and quickly leveraged his local fame into a spot in the rough-and-tumble arena of Chicago city politics. His first public office was as an assistant U.S. attorney. In 1916, he successfully ran for Alderman of the 23rd Ward, serving six years on the city council before successfully running for a spot on the Superior Court bench in Cook County in 1922.

Wally Steffen, during his time as a standout quarterback at the University of Chicago,

Steffen's active, high-profile life and career in Chicago more than proved his capacity for success and extraordinary accomplishment and was certainly more than enough to keep any man busy. However, it was not adequate for Steffen. In 1914, he agreed to do something never attempted before. He accepted an appointment to be the head coach of the football team of the Carnegie Institute of Technology, situated nearly 500 miles to the east, in Pittsburgh—a job he would perform largely from Chicago. In doing this, he became the first, and possibly only, long-distance coach in college football history.

During an era where part-time coaches were very much the norm, Steffen's arrangement with Carnegie was truly unique. From Sunday through Wednesday each autumn, Steffen communicated practice instructions and game plans from Chicago to Robert Waddell, his primary assistant coach. Waddell then implemented Steffen's plans and ran the daily practices and team activities from Sunday through Thursday. By late Thursday, Steffen would arrive via rail in time to preside over the Friday practice and the Saturday game. Each week on Sunday, the cycle began anew.

Since taking over in 1914, his Tech teams were far more respectable than those before, but with few exceptions, his teams still generally struggled to crack five wins in a season. However, as the fall of 1926 approached, Steffen had reason to be optimistic. First, his team was loaded with veterans of the previous year's varsity team and led by the unanimously selected captain, Lloyd Yoder, and senior running back Bill Donohue. Yoder, an extremely productive lineman, was an accomplished leader both on and off the field. His work on the line anchored a remarkable defense that would go on to rack up seven shutouts over the coming season. "Wild Bill" Donohue was a solid anchor in the backfield, known for his ability to execute the end run and being an exceptional open-field runner.

Second, Steffen had a dominant group of sophomores moving up to the varsity squad. The leader among them was Howard Harpster from Akron, Ohio, who would immediately start at quarterback upon joining the varsity and stay there for three full years. Right behind Harpster was Letzelter, who would quickly settle into the fullback role due to his ability to produce yardage through the center of the line and his versatility as an open-field runner and receiver. Joining them was Anthony Sweet of McKees Rocks, Letzelter's roommate, who quickly made his name as a formidable end, particularly when playing on the defensive side of the ball.

In late August, Steffen took a month-long "vacation" from his judicial duties in Chicago to kick off his preseason football camp, which began two weeks before the start of classes. They pointed toward their first game against Thiel at the beginning of October. The primary question facing them: How well would the upstart, record-breaking yearlings from 1925 gel with senior varsity veterans in rounding out the new 1926 Carnegie eleven?

ON OCTOBER 2, 1926 the Skibos took to the field with the same hope that accompanies opening games of all sports. Letzelter, as anticipated, joined Harpster and Donohue in the backfield as a fullback. Under Steffen's scheme, this called for Letzelter to be as effective in blocking behind the line as he was at running the ball.

The game started slow, with each team attempting to gain the upper hand. Cyril's only touch during that quarter was a 10-yard run for a first down. Beyond that, he was quiet, and so was the scoreboard. As the contest entered the second period, the game was a scoreless tie.

As the second quarter began, things started to pick up. On Cyril's first touch, he carried a Thiel defender five yards on

Cyril carries a defender on his back while running the ball in his first Varsity game with Carnegie Tech, vs. Thiel

his back for a significant gain; two plays later, he executed his first college pass, throwing for four more yards. Both plays contributed to the first scoring drive of the game, where Harpster plunged across the line to give Tech a 6-0 lead. On the very next Carnegie possession, Cyril had three carries for 13 yards in setting up yet another score, making the lead 12-0 at the half.

However, it was in the third quarter that Letzelter came alive. On the first possession of the second half, Letzelter carried the ball four times for 23 yards and the third touchdown of the day, which he followed up with by kicking the extra point. The lead was now 19 points.

After the Carnegie defense had held, Harpster looked to Letzelter on first down. The surprisingly fast Letzelter, who to that point had spent most of his time throwing his body in front of Thiel defenders, quickly cracked off a run of 40 yards, advancing the ball into the Thiel red zone. After a few plays, Letzelter's number was called again, and he burst through the line for his second consecutive touchdown. Cyril missed the extra point, so the lead sat at 25-0.

One can only speculate at what might have come next, but on the very next possession Letzelter was injured on a two-yard carry and forced out of the game to the wild applause of the Carnegie fans.

Notably for the Carnegie men, in running up a 42-0 victory over Thiel, five of the six touchdowns scored by Carnegie were by four freshmen: Harpster, English, Stauffer, and Letzelter. However, it was Cyril who decidedly led the team that day, according to reporter T. C. Youll:

> *Letzelter, a 180-pound fullback, was foremost in the Carnegie attack and left a trail of battered and bruised Thiel players in his wake. His steady hammering early in the game gradually wore down Thiel's light, forward wall and in the third period, when Carnegie cut loose with a dazzling drive, Letzelter ran wild . . . Its backs began to rip off long and consistent gains, with Letzelter in the van.*

In under three quarters, Letzelter had introduced himself to the college world with 12 carries for 96 yards, and 13 points.

The following week Cyril picked up where he left off, amassing 80 running yards in the first quarter as the Skibos ran up the score on tiny Adrian at Forbes Field in Pittsburgh. Running as if fired from a gun, Cyril stacked up runs of 11, 39, 7, 3, 10, and 10 yards on his first six carries. Perhaps due to his lingering injury, or maybe because Carnegie clearly outmatched their opponent, Cyril and most of the other starters exited the game midway through the second quarter. His final line on the day was eleven carries for 91 yards—an 8.2-yard average—and he converted three extra points in helping the team run up a 47-0 score. The game was a final tune-up before their first genuine test of the season against perennial rival Washington & Jefferson College.

The clash with W&J (as they were known) took place on a neutral field at a brand-new municipal stadium in Johnstown, Pennsylvania. While the game was hard fought, the result was a disappointing loss. Anchored by the massively sized and exceedingly talented fullback Hill Amos, the Presidents were able to overcome an early Tech touchdown to win 14-6. Amos ran amok, scoring both touchdowns, including one on a 90-yard return of a Harpster punt.

Cyril Letzelter strikes a pose for a promotional photo as a member of the Carnegie Varsity team

Of greater concern for Cyril was his first-half fumble—his third in two weeks—that led to W&J's first score. Despite his ball-handling challenges, Letz still found ways to contribute, including a 40-yard carry and a 20-yard reception early in the game. Nevertheless, the season's early momentum seemed in danger of stalling out with only a week to prepare for the "Steel City Championship" rivalry between Tech and its neighbor a few blocks west on Forbes Street, the University of Pittsburgh.

WITH THE SEASON nearing its midpoint, the 2-1 Skibos undoubtedly felt the outcome of their rivalry game against Pitt could set the tone for the remainder of their season. The stakes of the competition were always unusually high for Tech. Local sportswriter Max E. Hannum of the *Pittsburgh Press* once referred to the University of Pittsburgh as Carnegie Tech's "most ancient and most bitter rival." A poor performance would do more than hurt the team's record; it would also strike at the confidence of the sophomore-heavy team.

The spectacle of the city rivalry, played in the gigantic (for its period) Pitt Stadium to a crowd of approximately 50,000, was an event in every sense of the word. Both teams' marching bands took turns entertaining the crowd in the hour leading up to kickoff. World Heavyweight Boxing Champion Gene Tunney was on hand to preside over the opening coin toss, trailed everywhere by a bevy of news photographers and reporters.

Once the game began, however, it wasn't even close. Tech staked out an early lead when senior halfback Bill Donohoe scored on a spectacular 56-yard pass reception from Harpster in the first period and never looked back. Donohoe put another six on the board sprinting around the left end of the Pitt defense in the second quarter. Two placekicks by Cyril made the score 14-0 at halftime, a score that held for the rest of the day.

The result was such a surprise to national observers that it received a special write-up in the *New York Times*. However, for Cyril, though the victory was undoubtedly sweet, his performance in the game itself was limited. Beyond his two placekicks, he found his ability to penetrate the Pitt line mostly stifled and was left to make his mark on the defensive side of the ball, where he broke up several Pitt pass attempts.

However, his lack of standout performance against Pitt was the exception, not the rule. He bounced back the following week in Detroit, playing in such horrific conditions that only 4,000 came out to see the game. In a torrential rainstorm, playing on a muddy field that was reportedly ankle-deep, Cyril alone accounted for over half the team's yardage from scrimmage and produced the only points of the day, with a touchdown and extra point in the third period.

However, the knock against Tech historically was that their teams tended to play their best in October and fold down the stretch. A 6-0 loss against New York at Yankee Stadium on November 1 only helped fuel that narrative. The loss, while a setback, still allowed the team's stellar defense to shine. Trapped by bad field position nearly all of the game, the Skibos still kept New York out of the end zone, and Cyril contributed at least one touchdown-preventing fumble recovery. Their blowout victory against tiny Juniata the next week—where the starters got a break as the second team ran up a 52-0 win—did little to prove that the team had reversed the November doldrums.

With only two games remaining, the consensus was that the November 20 game at home against West Virginia was their last realistic chance to notch a win. Knute Rockne was currently fielding his most powerful Notre Dame team to date, and the late November matchup between the two was considered nothing more than a tune-up for the Irish before they traveled to their first ever matchup against the University of Southern

California—a likely contest between unbeaten teams expected to decide the national champion.

Against West Virginia, Carnegie Tech came through unscathed, notching their third shutout in four games with a 20-0 win. Cyril contributed a 25-yard touchdown run and two extra points, as well as snagging an interception on the defensive side with a subsequent return that set up the second Tech scoring drive. As the game ended that afternoon, before a crowd of at least 11,000, the Skibos has notched six wins for only the third time in two decades. By any measure, and regardless of the coming week's outcome against the most potent team in the country, for Carnegie Tech the season was already a smashing success.

The Underdogs

By the end of 1925, Knute Rockne was already a living legend. In eight years as head coach of the Fighting Irish, he had amassed an astounding 65 wins with only six losses. His "Four Horsemen" memorialized by the prose of Grantland Rice had captured the imagination of the nation barely two years prior. And late into the 1926 season, he and his program showed no signs of letting up.

With eight games completed in the 1926 season, the Irish were an unstoppable machine. They opened the season hosting tiny Beloit College, running up the score 77-0 in their win. A week later they traveled to Minnesota, where they gave up only one touchdown in conquering their northern opponent by a score of 20-7.

After that, Rockne's squad went on a six-game run without allowing their opposition to score a single point. The Irish racked up shutouts against Penn State, Northwestern, Georgia Tech, Indiana, Drake, and the then-perennial powerhouse Army. Over those six games, the Irish outscored their opposition 100-0.

By this point, it was clear that Rockne's wrecking crew was on track to a season-ending showdown against the University of Southern California two weeks hence that was likely to result in Rockne's third (or fourth, depending on how one counted) national championship. No one knew that this first meeting with USC, which Rockne had worked years to schedule, would also grow into one of the greatest college football rivalries in history.

146

Rockne, always shrewd when it came to scheduling, had planned two lightweight games between his big contests against Army and USC. This popular tactic of scheduling "breathers" allowed teams to stay sharp while playing a matchup where the outcome was essentially predetermined. In this case, Notre Dame had already dispatched Drake comfortably 21-0. Only Carnegie Tech stood between the all-important matchup between the Irish and Southern California.

Carnegie had a well-established reputation as a tune-up for Rockne. The year 1926 would be the fifth year in a row that the two teams had met. Notre Dame hadn't just won every meeting to that point; they dominated the Skibos by a combined score of 111-19.

The series was so overwhelmingly lopsided that, as the game approached, rumors ran rampant that Rockne intended to keep his first team starters at home to rest for the battle with USC. In fact, those tales grew so loud that on the Monday before the game, Rockne himself felt compelled to send a telegram to Tech's Athletic Director, Clarence "Buddy" Overend, to set the record straight. "We are pointing for your game Saturday and will give you all we have," said Rockne.

Rockne's promise, however, was only half accurate. While all the Notre Dame players made the trip, Rockne himself did not. Instead, he elected to attend the Army-Navy game in Chicago. Contrary to the legend claiming Rockne was just scouting both teams, in reality, he missed the game at the behest of Christy Walsh. Walsh was the first nationally recognized sports agent and represented such famous athletic luminaries as Babe Ruth. In a letter to Walsh discussing the trip to Chicago,

Rockne wrote, "The game in Pittsburgh will not be important enough. . . . I can (put) it in charge of someone else."

Walsh's idea was to bring Rockne, Pop Warner of Stanford, and Yale's Tad Jones together for the historic event. The Army-Navy game was not only the biggest contest of the year, but the event also heralded the christening of a new sports venue in Chicago, Soldier Field. Once together, the legendary coaches would write a newspaper article about the Army-Navy game and then select an All-American football team to be published in papers nationwide. All the coaches, of course, would receive compensation for their efforts. For the Carnegie Tech game, Rockne left the team in the hands of his assistant, Hunk Anderson.

Even though Rockne was not traveling east to Pittsburgh, another man from Chicago was headed in the right direction. As Rockne stayed behind in Chicago, Wally Steffen, the full-time Cook County Judge and weekend coach of the Skibos, boarded the rails and headed east to his waiting team, knowing that, if nothing else, Rockne had handed his team a motivational opportunity for the ages. Steffen planned to take full advantage.

At dinner with his team the night before the game, Steffen wasted no time in reminding his players that the papers said they had no chance and that by skipping the game, Rockne had disrespected them despite the fact that Carnegie had scored 19 points against Rockne's famous "Four Horsemen" in 1924.

Steffen also knew that Notre Dame would likely employ its often-used strategy of starting the game with the second-string team—what Rockne called his "shock troops." This tactic had been used previously to great effect by the Irish as a way to

148

lure opponents into a false sense of complacency and give the first team a chance to observe their opponent's game plan for signs of weakness. After several possessions, the first team would enter the game fresh and fierce and ready to dominate.

Instead of treating this as a standard Notre Dame tactic, Steffen added it to the narrative he was building for his team about the contest. In the locker room before the game, Steffen said to his team, "Men, Knute Rockne thinks you so poor as football players that he's starting his second string against you, and he's so sure he'll win, he's not even here. . . . He's in Chicago watching Army and Navy play some real football."

By game time, the Skibos were breathing fire.

THE AFTERNOON IN Pittsburgh on November 27, 1926, was cold, cloudy, and gray, with a light dusting of snow blowing in from the west. Looming large between the campuses of the University of Pittsburgh and Carnegie Tech, in the Oakland neighborhood, lay Forbes Field. The seventeen-year-old, three-tiered stadium was the first of its kind built in the United States, relying on concrete and steel to hold extraordinarily large crowds and to increase its longevity. Primarily the home of professional baseball's Pittsburgh Pirates, the stadium had also hosted University of Pittsburgh home football games until 1924, when that team moved into the larger Pitt Stadium just a few blocks away. While the Skibos didn't have nearly the draw of Pitt, they continued to use Forbes Field as their home location for football, which was fortunate, as the national popularity of Notre Dame demanded a large venue.

The scheduled game time was 2:00 p.m. sharp, but that didn't prevent a bit of preliminary psychological gamesmanship. Notre Dame hit the field at 1:45 p.m. for warmups before briefly returning to the locker rooms, expecting to make their grand entrance. However, when they returned to the field 10 minutes later, the Skibos had yet to take the field. As the Carnegie players began to take the field barely a minute later, Notre Dame slipped back into their locker room and made Tech and the record crowd of 45,000 wait just a few more minutes before the presumptive national champions took the field.

Notre Dame won the toss and, as expected, Hunk Anderson sent the second team "shock troops" to take the field while the first team stayed on the sideline to preserve energy and observe their opponent. However, the Irish quickly got off to a rocky start, with John Niemec needing three attempts at kickoff to get the ball properly into play. On the third attempt Tech's veteran back Bill Donohue fielded the kick and returned it to the Carnegie 32-yard line.

Two plays later, Tech was in Irish territory thanks to a 10-yard run by C. J. Mefort and a 15-yard penalty against Notre Dame for unnecessary roughness. On the next play, Letzelter got his first chance of the game and broke a 5-yard run off the right tackle that was brought back due to penalty. His next chance was on third down and four, where he gained only one yard on a fake double-pass play. Tech quarterback Howard Harpster then launched a booming punt that pinned Notre Dame deep on their own 13.

The Tech defense then took the field and quickly proceeded to make a statement of its own. After holding the Irish to 8 yards in three downs, Saul Mielziner broke through the line on fourth down and blocked Johnny Niemec's punt. Carnegie recovered just 26 yards away from the Irish goal line.

Notre Dame's defense stiffened. Carnegie, bound and determined to get past the goal line, gave the ball first to Letzelter, who picked up two through the middle of the line, and then twice to Mefort for a combined 5 yards.

Sitting at the Notre Dame 19-yard line, Tech was in easy range of a quick three points due to the talented drop-kicking skills of sophomore Howard Harpster. Instead, Steffen made a puzzling call to try to pick up three more yards on fourth down to keep the drive going. It did not work. Mefort with his third straight carry hit an unforgiving Irish wall, and Carnegie's early momentum came to a screeching halt.

As the snow fell and the shadows grew, the game settled into a form of trench warfare. Over the remainder of the first quarter, there was only one more first down, by Notre Dame on an 18-yard pass from Riley to John Niemec that brought the Irish to midfield. Yet once again, the defense hardened, and Notre Dame was forced to punt.

There was evidence that this was exactly the type of game Wally Steffen wanted to see at this point. Well aware of Notre Dame's "shock troops" strategy due to scouting reports from the Irish's previous two games, in the first quarter Steffen twice had Harpster punt on third down, including once right after a play where Letzelter had ripped off another 5-yard run. Steffen's plan was to minimize early mistakes, consciously hold back his playbook, and try to keep the Notre Dame second team pinned back in their own territory until the first team entered the fray.

The second quarter began with yet another third down punt by Harpster that placed the Irish at their own 20. After a 1-yard gain and a fumble that they barely recovered, it was the Irish's turn to cut their losses and also punt on third down.

The pattern continued with the Skibos. The next series of downs saw Tech unable to advance the ball at all and further take two penalties that moved them backward 10 yards, Harpster fell back to punt yet again. However, an unnecessary roughness call on Notre Dame gave the ball back to the Skibos with a first down near midfield.

At this point, Hunk Anderson had seen enough. He pulled the trigger and switched out the second team for the first team, and a mighty roar erupted from the legions of Irish fans at Forbes Field.

It would not last.

As soon as the first team for the Irish hit the field, the eleven men of Carnegie Tech opened the throttle and the playbook they had been holding in reserve. In quick succession, Tech started eating up large portions of the field: another Mefort run of 15 yards, a Harpster pass to Donohue for 21, and a Letzelter run for 5 that set up a 15-yard scoring run by Donohue. In seven quick plays, the Skibos had sprinted down half of the field, embarrassed the vaunted Notre Dame first team, and put the first points on the board. Carnegie Tech 6, Notre Dame 0.

Letzelter's kick for the extra point bounced off the goalpost—no good. But if the Irish took this as a good sign it did not show. A clearly rattled Notre Dame immediately fumbled the kickoff from Harpster, falling on it just in time to maintain possession deep in their own territory. Three plays

152

and eight yards later, Notre Dame was lining up to punt again. Only this time, the energized Tech line broke through the All-American Irish line and blocked its second punt of the day, and once again, within minutes, Carnegie was lining up less than 20 yards away from another touchdown.

In short order, Harpster completed a 15-yard pass to Mefort, setting the ball up in the center of the field on the Irish 3-yard line. With two successive runs up the center, Letzelter gained the yards and scored the second touchdown. And this time, his extra point
did not miss.

Very quietly, Cy Letzelter was putting together another exceptional performance. Never flashy, he was now leading the offense in number of carries and total points scored, and had produced several key defensive plays on the other side of the ball. In the space of a few short minutes, what had been fruitless defensive struggle became an astonishing 13-point lead for the underdogs. In under two quarters, the Skibos put more points on the board than all of the Irish's previous opponents that year combined.

With halftime looming, Notre Dame buckled down and put together its best drive of the afternoon, gaining two first downs and moving the ball from their own 25 to the Carnegie Tech 40-yard line. With the clock running down, the Irish elected to throw on fourth down. Batted down by E. H. Gielfus, Carnegie Tech took possession on downs. Harpster executed a quick, 2-yard run and then led his team to the locker room, leaving a shocked Irish team and a crazed Pittsburgh crowd in its wake.

PERHAPS IF ROCKNE had attended the game, he would have used the break to remotivate his team, make necessary coaching

The Touchdown That Was Heard All Over America

Cyril Letzelter, buried at the bottom of the pile, is shown scoring Carnegie Tech's second touchdown of the day against Notre Dame in this news clip from one of the Ohio Valley local newspapers

adjustments, and send his men screaming back onto the field with a single-minded purpose. As it was, it was not even clear that the Irish knew they were in serious trouble. Despite the stunning first half, contemporary news stories spoke of the still-calm confidence at halftime of the Notre Dame fans present, and the fact that bookmakers in the stands actually increased the odds that the Irish would mount the comeback that everyone seemed to know was coming. Despite entering the final half of a game where they were behind by 13 points, it still seemed unthinkable that this tiny afterthought of a football program could hold on and produce an upset for the ages.

And for a time, it seemed they might be right. Bill Donahue fumbled the kickoff opening the second half and barely fell on the ball in time to maintain possession at his 15-yard line. Three plays produced only 2 yards of offense and an offsides penalty, pushing them farther back toward their own goal. This time, when Harpster punted on third down, it seemed like a reasonable attempt to avoid a devastating mistake.

However, the Irish, despite having taken over on the Carnegie Tech 41-yard line, were unable to take full advantage. After gaining 6 quick yards in two plays and finally getting to the edge of scoring territory, Irish co-captain and right halfback Tom Heardon fumbled, setting off a wild attempt to recover the ball that ended when Christie Flanagan smothered the pigskin. Notre Dame was then called for holding—a 15-yard penalty—which pushed them well out of scoring range. A solid punt pinned the Skibos inside their own 15-yard line.

Steffens offense continued to appear in neutral. His initial strategy of cycling the ball between Donohue, Mefort, and Letzelter was producing little yardage and no opportunity for any of his talented backs to develop a rhythm. Only penalties against the Irish were allowing Carnegie to advance at all.

The next Irish possession produced a critical break. On second down, Carnegie team captain Bill Yoder intercepted a forward pass and was tackled at the Notre Dame 35-yard line, already well within Harpster's drop-kick range. After three quick plays that produced only 1 yard, Harpster capitalized on the Irish turnover with a booming field goal that was said to have cleared the bar by more than 10 yards. Despite a lackluster second-half performance to that point, Carnegie somehow added to their lead. It was now Carnegie Tech 16, Notre Dame 0.

On the very next possession for Notre Dame, again on second down, Carnegie's Bill Yoder capitalized on yet another

Irish turnover and recovered the ball on the opposing 28-yard line. Thanks to a Letzelter run of 4 yards, Harpster was inside the 25-yard line when he drop-kicked another field goal, putting the lead at 19-0.

At this point, the Notre Dame partisans had to be panicked. Despite their defense holding Tech to only 10 yards in the half so far (7 of which came on Letzelter's only three touches in the period), they had seen their deficit grow by 6 more points.

But the performance of the Notre Dame defense continued to give the Irish hope. If they could stop the turnovers and give their offense a chance to find its rhythm, the game was still in reach. And a 29-yard completion on a pass by Christie Flanagan at the end of the third period fired their hopes once again, reminding the crowd of the potent Notre Dame offense.

And so the final quarter began with Notre Dame quickly moving the ball by ground and by air, completing another 28-yard pass to get them to the 1-foot line of Carnegie Tech. A quick sack on the next play pushed the Irish back 4 yards, giving the Skibos some much-needed breathing room. They called a timeout to get ready for the goal line stand.

It was now second down and goal on the Tech 4-yard line. A handoff to Harry O'Boyle moved the ball again to the 1-foot line. Notre Dame would have two attempts to cover 12 inches and potentially bring the game quickly back into reach with close to a full quarter yet to play.

Quarterback Charley Riley made the first attempt on a sneak behind the mighty Notre Dame line, but Carnegie held. The first attempt covered 8 inches and left 4 more to go. With so much on riding on this critical fourth down, it was no surprise that the Irish put the ball into the hands of their All-American star halfback, Christie Flanagan. It was a surprise when Tech breached the great Irish line and sacked Flanagan for a loss.

Carnegie took over immediately on downs, and Harpster, standing in his own end zone, wasted no time in attempting to get the team out of danger. He punted on first down, pushing the Irish back 30 yards. A fumble recovery on the play by Bill Donohue was run back for what appeared to be another Carnegie touchdown, but the ball was called back due to unnecessary roughness, and Notre Dame took the ball in hand again on the Carnegie 20. The threat remained.

On the very next play, Tech's fortunes turned when Charley Riley threw an interception at the line of scrimmage, and the offense returned to the field.

At this point, Steffen had seen enough. With every second bringing them closer to victory, he needed to keep the ball moving and keep the clock running. And as the fans in the Carnegie section chanted "give it to Letz" loud enough to be heard over the radio broadcast, Steffen turned to the only Carnegie back that hadn't lost yardage all day: nineteen-year-old sophomore Cy Letzelter.

Unlike earlier in the game, when the Carnegie backs rarely saw the ball twice in a set of downs, on this critical possession they rode Letzelter down the field as the young, powerful halfback started tearing apart the Notre Dame line anchored by All-American Bud Boeringer. On what would ultimately be Tech's final drive of the day, Letzelter carried the ball ten times for 35 yards, never failing to advance the ball, moving the line an average of about 4 yards a clip and producing three consecutive first downs.

By the time Carnegie finally faced a fourth down, Letzelter had led his team to the Notre Dame 11-yard line and had nearly milked the game clock dry. Even though Notre Dame managed to block Harpster's attempt at a third field goal, the Irish were broken, and the Skibos of Carnegie Tech had produced an earthquake in the world of college football.

THREE PLAYS LATER, the game clock expired, and the crowd of 45,000 began to pour onto the field, some carrying the Carnegie eleven off the field on their shoulders. Others had a more concrete objective in mind, as was described the following day:

> *Through the seething mass that wildly charged onto the playing surface at Forbes Field yesterday when the field judge's last whistle sounded the death knell of Notre Dame's championship hopes, came one small party with a definite objective. . . . They made straight for the south goal, and before a blue coat could interfere, they had dismantled the uprights and the cross bar, and started an impromptu parade of their own.*

While it is uncertain if this was a first in football history, the media treated it as an exceptionally rare event, sniffing, "Never before, or not in recent years, had the enthusiasm of any football crowd approached that stage where it was necessary to tear down the goal posts."

The following day's newspapers reacted with predictable shock, giving the upset equal billing to the epic Army-Navy game—the very game Rockne attended instead—that ended in a tie and was discussed as one of the greatest football games ever played. A surprising aspect of the coverage was the emphasis on the roles of Tech seniors Donohue and Yoder and the quarterback Howard Harpster, and the secondary billing given to Letzelter. This was despite the fact that Letzelter led the team that day in carries, rushing yardage, and points scored, and played such a critical role in finally getting the Carnegie offense in gear at a time when the Irish began playing their best offensive football of the day. It was a dynamic that would often reoccur as the Carnegie eleven gained prominence over the next several years.

Regardless, no one could deny that it was a game of historic importance. Carnegie Tech rushed a special, eight-page edition of their quarterly magazine, the *Carnegie Alumnus*, based solely on the game—complete with game detail, analysis, public reactions, reports of telegrams sent from all over the world, and even poetry written to honor the team and its incredible accomplishment. It's no surprise that sports historians have termed the game an "upset of stupendous proportions," and it is still considered by many to be the greatest upset in the annals of college football history.

But perhaps the most incisive, if politically incorrect, take came from the famous humorist Will Rogers, who attended the game and later wrote to the *New York Times*, "It's the worst thing that has hit Indiana since the Klansmen run out of sheets."

Hamilton Fish's War

While the delirious fans of Carnegie Tech pulled down the goalposts at Forbes Field in Pittsburgh, Knute Rockne watched as a new stadium in Chicago was christened by what would be labeled at the time as "the game of the century." Before an enormous crowd of over 110,000 people, the two service academies met on Soldier Field and battled to an epic 6-6 tie. The next morning, Tech's upset of the Irish and the Army-Navy game battled for space on the same front pages of sports sections across the country.

But brimming just below the surface of the ultra-competitive service academy rivalry was a long-simmering controversy that was just about to burst open.

The annual gridiron battle between the nation's two predominant service academies was known to stir particularly passionate emotions. Just before the turn of the century, the series had taken a four-year hiatus because of growing concerns in the War Department over the bad blood being created between students and alumni of the two academies, who ultimately needed to be able to work together on the battlefield. When the series resumed in 1899, efforts were made to de-escalate passions by scheduling the games on a neutral field, usually in either New York or Philadelphia. That tradition continues to this day.

Nevertheless, a long-aggravating point of contention continued between the two academies over the issue of player eligibility.

The Naval Academy at Annapolis hewed closer to the emerging standard in the college football world: three-year eligibility. Under this guideline, potential players could play for only three varsity seasons, and they had to successfully complete at least one year of successful coursework before being allowed on the varsity team. However, while this standard was quickly coming into broad acceptance, it was by no means a rule.

The United States Military Academy at West Point, on the other hand, had no such standard. As an institution that took pride in its manner of breaking its cadets down and then rebuilding them through vigorous academic and physical training, the idea of inequitable treatment of cadets, particularly within a single cadet class, was contrary to the very ethos of the institution. Not only did West Point allow incoming freshmen, or "yearlings," to play all four years, they also accepted new cadets who had already earned degrees—and significant football experience—from other four-year universities.

The West Point position was that everyone who received a valid appointment to the academy—which could only be received via congressional or presidential appointment—entered the academy on equal terms. A cadet with a college degree was every bit the plebe as a cadet without a high school degree. This mindset applied to sports as well. Once you entered the Point, you participated, and you were judged as if you had never existed prior to your arrival. In theory, this meant no one was to receive special treatment.

In practice, this meant that boosters who cared deeply about football, and who had the ability to swing an appointment to West Point, could help recruit well-experienced college players to Army, where they could extend their football careers and be placed on a career path as an officer and a gentleman.

While Navy had raised the issue of differing player eligibility standards as far back as 1903, it was only after the Great War, when the troops returned and the series resumed, that Annapolis began to really press the issue. Contemporary reports suggest that tensions increasingly grew as Navy failed to notch a single win against Army after the 1921 season. Army, of course, saw the complaining as a case of sour grapes, pointing out the three-game winning streak Navy notched against Army from 1919 to 1921 and the epic tie of 1926 as evidence that the teams were still very closely matched.

Even so, Army took what they felt was a significant step to address the controversy by announcing weeks before the 1926 game that, starting with the following year, West Point would formally adopt a one-year rule prohibiting academy freshmen from playing varsity sports. While this was progress, the new rule did nothing to limit participation for players who had prior college playing experience and therefore was seen by Navy as missing the point.

And so, in June of the following year, Naval Academy officials made a move to bring the matter to a head by formally adopting a three-year-maximum eligibility policy and stating that Navy would only schedule future games with programs that adhered to the same standard. This immediately raised tensions between the two camps, but because the two programs were already engaged in a multi-year scheduling agreement, a formal break in relations did not appear to be on the immediate horizon, and the 1927 game occurred as planned.

However, Navy was about to play its trump card. Starting with the 1927 game, the two programs operated under a four-year scheduling agreement that allowed terms to be subject to revision by either party, and for 1928, it was Navy's turn to draw up the contract. When the draft contract for the 1928 contract was submitted to West Point, it came with the following clause: "It is mutually agreed by the Superintendents . . . that no contestant shall take part in this game on either team who has had three years' experience in intercollegiate football . . . to include participation in intercollegiate football while at either academy or any other accredited credited college or university."

Ominously, the proposed agreement included was language stating that rejection of the eligibility feature would represent rejection of the contract as a whole. The gauntlet had been thrown.

It is not known if Navy expected Army to negotiate further over this clause, but in mid-December of 1927, Major General Edwin Winans of West Point replied in clear and forceful fashion. Not only did Army reject the eligibility proposal, but it specifically noted that since Navy's insistence that rejection of the eligibility clause would constitute a rejection of the contract in whole, they assumed that it was Navy's wish to be released from its obligation to play Army—a wish Army would honor. Then, West Point released its response to the media in New York before officials in Annapolis had even received a copy. The following day, Navy issued a statement that suggested Army's response indicated that West Point opposed a fair contest, and with that, football relations between the two academies were severed.

Enter Congressman Hamilton Fish.

HAMILTON FISH WAS a man who saw red.

A 1910 graduate of Harvard, he was a hyper-competitive man who took out his aggression on the gridiron as the team captain of the Crimsons. Selected twice as an All-American, he was inducted into the College Football Hall of Fame in 1954. And his passion for football—particularly Harvard football—was so intense that in 1970, when his own sister died, he demanded (successfully) that the date of her funeral be changed so as not to conflict with that year's Harvard-Yale game.

His grandchildren tell stories of how, as a spectator, he often had to be restrained from leaving the stands during games in order to give the Harvard coaches a piece of his mind—even as his age approached one hundred years.

His fierceness went beyond sports. A former politician, he once counted Franklin Delano Roosevelt as one of his great friends. In fact, FDR himself offered to help jump-start Fish's political career by engineering him as his replacement in the New York State Senate when he left to become assistant secretary of the Navy in 1913—this despite the fact that they came from different parties.

Their friendship lasted until 1932, when FDR became president and Fish's congressional role as the ranking Republican of the House Rules and Foreign Affairs Committees—and thereby opponent of nearly all of FDR's initiatives—earned him the distinction of being personally barred from the White House by the president himself.

His loyalty to his party—his team, so to speak—was

such that in 1986, when his grandson and namesake ran for Congress as a Democrat, the staunch Republican all but branded him a communist and announced his intent to personally campaign against him.

Hamilton Fish was a man who took sides.

As a young Crimson, Fish only got to play the team of the United States Military Academy once, during his senior season of 1909. The long-running series between the two teams

had been on hiatus in 1907 and 1908 to allow the Naval Academy a shot at taking down the dominant Harvard program. Neither academy pulled it off. In 1909, Army fell to the Crimsons 9-0—the fifth consecutive time they had been shut out.

Congressman Hamilton Fish, pictured in 1919

In fact, in these early days of football, the military academy teams were no match for the mighty Harvard program. Even after the reforms of 1906 had limited the flying wedges and other momentum-based styles of play pioneered and favored by Harvard, the Crimsons were still a major force to be reckoned with.

Between 1895 and 1910, Harvard and Army met 12 times on the gridiron, and 12 times the Cadets fell, and they fell hard. Every single game except one was a shutout, and even the 1902 game, where Army managed to put 6 points on the board, Harvard still bested them with 14 points of their own.

WHILE HAMILTON FISH didn't know it, by the time the 1926

season rolled around, Harvard football was already beginning a decline from which it would never really recover. Though Harvard and its companion East Coast, Ivy League teams had sat atop the football world for some decades since the game's inception, the postwar explosion of the sport permanently upended this dynamic.

Upon the return from the Great War, the Harvard men were able to field two straight undefeated teams in 1919 and 1920, followed by strong seasons in 1921 and 1922. Those four years, however, would be enough time for traditional also-rans to begin building up more competitive programs of their own, and as a result, starting in 1923 the Harvard program would struggle to post more than a handful of wins each season for decades.

Viewed through the prism of 1926, however, Fish could be excused for believing a few tough seasons were just a blip on the radar for his beloved Harvard. But, just like that man who decades later would postpone his sister's funeral for the Harvard-Yale game, Fish's all-encompassing dedication to his alma mater's football team would cause him to fulminate and ruminate over the state of the program at length, looking for explanations.

Before long, he would come to focus on the problem of proselytizing in college football, and he would come to view the Army program as public offender number one.

AS THE YEAR 1928 progressed, the prevailing thought was that Army and Navy would find a way to iron out their differences and find a way to meet on the gridiron during the

166

football season. To the surprise of many, that did not occur. There was no game in 1928.

However, Army did add a new team to its 1928 schedule. It was an old rival whom they had not met on the gridiron for 18 years. A team upon which they had barely been able to score over a dozen contests dating back before the turn of the twentieth century. That team was the Harvard Crimsons.

When they met on October 20 of that year, it was the third game of the season for the Crimsons, and they looked strong. Coming into the game, they had shut out their previous two opponents by a combined score of 50-0. Hopes for the season were undoubtedly high.

So imagine the reaction when that proud alumnus and congressman, Hamilton Fish, watched his beloved Crimsons get torched 15-0 on their home field by the Cadets of Army.

Perhaps the wound of the loss would not have festered, except Harvard went on to have a fairly impressive season. Harvard fell only one other time that year, to Pittsburgh by a score of 7-0. The 15 points scored by Army that season represented more than half of the points the Crimsons gave up that entire year. From the perspective of the passionate alumnus Hamilton Fish, Army had derailed a great Harvard season.

And they had done it, in his point of view, by cheating—by recruiting experienced college graduates to give themselves an unfair advantage over teams like Harvard.

Hamilton Fish was enraged. He was also a member of Congress. And it was only a matter of time before he would find a way to make his voice heard.

IT WAS NEARLY 7 months before Fish finally saw an opportunity to use his official position to launch his quixotic campaign to force West Point to change its eligibility rules. As the congressman whose district included West Point, Fish decided he was in a unique position to apply pressure for a deal that would get Army and Navy to schedule a 1929 game.

The basis of the compromise, in Fish's mind, was that Army needed to stop cheating. His proposed "compromise" plan, which he submitted in writing to Secretary of War James W. Good on May 31, 1929, was noteworthy in several respects. Most notably, it called upon only West Point to make concessions, based on his sole opinion that Army's policy on player eligibility was clearly "unsportsmanlike"—a contention that was both inflammatory and hotly disputed by West Point officials.

Equally odd was Fish's insinuation that he was speaking for other major football programs, writing:

The fact that such colleges as Harvard, Yale, Notre Dame, Nebraska, and Stanford continue to play West Point does not mean that the colleges condone or accept the present West Point eligibility rules as being fair or consistent with the amateur regulations governing college football, but because the Army eleven is a big attraction to the public, especially when the cadet corps is permitted to accompany the team.

However, with the exception of the fact that Fish included an unofficial statement from one Horatio S. White, an 1873 Harvard alumnus who had once served on the Harvard

Athletic Committee two decades prior, Fish produced no evidence that any of the named institutions formally agreed with or endorsed his position. In fact, there was ample evidence to the contrary.

Notre Dame, for example, was not only a strong supporter of the Army program (thanks in large part to its appreciation of Army's critical role in saving the football program from Fielding Yost's and the Big Ten's boycott of Notre Dame just fifteen years earlier), but Rockne's team had just beaten West Point for the sixth time in 8 games. Yale had only fallen to Army twice in six games, and both Stanford and Nebraska had played Army only once since the end of the Great War, with Stanford winning and Nebraska losing its contest.

In other words, the examples Fish gave, with the exception of Harvard, were teams that had tended to dominate the Cadets on the gridiron and had no obvious gripes with the program.

Fish's "compromise," such that it was, suggested that Army adopt a four-year eligibility rule that counted previous play at other schools—for example, a Cadet who had played two years in college could then only play two years at West Point. Fish's position was that this was a reasonable compromise because it still gave Army a slight advantage, as Navy operated with a three-year eligibility rule. All it asked of Annapolis was that Navy agree to play Army once the Cadets changed their eligibility standards.

It's not difficult to see why this proposal gained no traction.

Merits of the argument aside, it is truly astonishing in retrospect to consider Fish's actions here. Keep in mind that the

United States Military Academy was one of the most important institutions situated within Fish's congressional district. In this case, we see a sitting Congressman attempting a high-profile intervention with the secretary of war against the interests of the academy—his own constituency! To take such a provocative approach against such an important, in-district constituency indicates an extreme personal interest in the underlying issue.

This is especially remarkable when one considers that Fish had no special connection to Annapolis or the Navy, and his history to that point showed no special interest in the Army-Navy game. It also seems unlikely, given what is known about Fish's history of support for the Harvard football program, that Fish would have been so moved to action if the beneficiary were not his beloved Crimsons.

Rather, it seems clear that Fish was spurred to action in this case because he had felt the personal sting of defeat at the hands of Army's talent on the Crimsons' home gridiron in 1928.

Fish's proposal, of course, went nowhere. Army and Navy did not meet on the field in 1929. But while this particular battle may have been lost, Hamilton Fish's war was just beginning.

Rockne's Boswell

Nothing was more telling about the duplicity behind Hamilton Fish's initial moves against the West Point program than the fact that he championed programs, such as Notre Dame, that he claimed were at a competitive disadvantage due to the academy's ability to recruit older, more experienced players. The evidence indicated that the two programs were more evenly matched than Fish would have led people to believe.

A cursory review of Notre Dame's 1928 varsity squad is a bracing reminder that, despite Fish's arguments to the contrary, whatever patchwork of rules governing player eligibility existed in the late 1920s, at best they were far from comprehensive. For example, under the three-year rule adopted by West Point, combined with that institution's age limit of twenty-two or under to accept an appointment, the oldest player for Army in the most extreme of cases could never be more than twenty-six years old.

During that 1928 season Notre Dame, by contrast, counted twenty-eight-year old Jerry Ransavage as its oldest player, and the average age for the university's senior players exceeded twenty-three years old—nearly a full year older than one would expect for a basic college program accepting players straight from high school.

This inconsistency is not to say that Fish's critiques were entirely without merit. Rather, it illustrates how in the 1920s, the rules regarding player eligibility were still quite malleable. The best programs—including Notre Dame, Army, and others—had little trouble getting the best, most-experienced players onto the gridiron.

Adding to the irony of Fish comparing the two programs' approach to player eligibility is the fact that it was the exploits of one of the oldest players on Rockne's squad who ultimately decided the outcome of the 1928 Army–Notre Dame. The hero of that game was halfback Johnny Neimec, a twenty-three-year-old senior who hailed from Bellaire, Ohio. He was the very same Neimec to whom J. F. Mullaney had favorably compared Cyril back in 1924 when he named his young protégé to the All-Valley team as a sophomore.

The reason Neimec was still on the Irish squad at his age was that he had clearly been recruited by Notre Dame, even attending a Rockne-friendly preparatory school before heading to the university. Specifically, he took a detour after his high school graduation to play football at St. Edward's College in Austin, Texas—another Holy Cross order Catholic school started in 1872 by the same Father Edward Sorin who had founded the University of Notre Dame three decades before.

It is fair to assume that Neimec almost certainly owed his spot on the roster to one of Rockne's most famous "bird-dogs" of all, Bellaire native Francis Wallace. Given Wallace's historical role scouting the Ohio Valley for Rockne, it is improbable to imagine a hometown boy like Neimec headed to South Bend without the sponsorship of Wallace. Also, in future correspondence with Rockne, Wallace was known to compare potential recruits to Neimec, which seems to indicate Wallace felt a sense of pride regarding this particular Irish star.

In any event, Neimec's heroics in that famous Army–Notre Dame contest have been somewhat obscured over time

172

because the game itself now stands as one of the cornerstones of the great Notre Dame mythos, as it was immortalized years later in the Hollywood biopic *Knute Rockne: All American.*

The movie featured a young Ronald Reagan in his most memorable acting role. It dramatized that game where allegedly, at halftime, Knute Rockne delivered an impassioned speech to his players telling them the tale of the dying wish of former player George Gipp. According to lore, Gipp legendarily asked Rockne to implore the boys to go out and, in a game against Army, "win one for the Gipper."

IN 1928, THE story of George Gipp would have seemed an odd choice to inspire the Notre Dame eleven. Hardly a paragon of virtue, Gipp's real-life reputation was that of a gambling, hard-drinking, semi-professional athlete with a less-than-stellar academic record and a penchant for breaking the rules. According to Notre Dame historian Murray Sperber, in the postgame coverage of Rockne's halftime speech, "one wit later noted that 'it would have been much more like him (Gipp) to ask Rock to put down a bet for him some day when the Irish were a sure thing.'"

Though Gipp was a tremendous player, his memory had already faded from view behind Rockne's later triumphs with his Four Horsemen and other assorted giants of the 1920-era college game. At the time, the Protestant Gipp did not hold a special place either in the nation's consciousness or with the overwhelmingly Catholic fan base of Notre Dame. So why Gipp, and why now?

Sperber points out that in 1928, there was one journalist for whom Gipp remained a vivid hero, who had seen him play and had cheered his exploits: Francis Wallace. Moreover, two days before the 1928 game against Army, Wallace wrote a story for the New York *Daily News* emphasizing Gipp's role for Notre Dame against teams from West Point. In short, before the 1928 Notre Dame–Army contest, it was Wallace who reintroduced Gipp into the national conversation.

It might not have gotten much traction, as Wallace was already known as a writer who was very close to Rockne and the Notre Dame program. However, Wallace's article did not go unnoticed. Other sportswriters and newspapers, competing for attention, latched on to the Wallace story. The following day a far more credible journalist gave the Gipp legend an essential boost. In his column, W. O. McGeehan of the *New York Herald Tribune* called Gipp "the greatest individual football player I ever saw." With that, the stage was set to, as they say, "write the legend," which is just what he did.

Though Wallace had not been in the locker room, he broke the story of Rockne's halftime speech two days later based on the account of an eyewitness, Joe Byrne Jr. Headlined "Gipp's Ghost Beat Army," Wallace's report angered Rockne, likely due to his fear that the Gipp story he told would not stand up to scrutiny, nor would the increased attention on Gipp's character be particularly beneficial for the school.

To Rockne's great relief, however, Wallace's contemporary account never gained national traction. It was only later versions of the story, primarily from Rockne's posthumous autobiography and the memoirs of Grantland Rice, that spun the wider tale of Gipp's supposed deathbed conversion to Catholicism, his alleged request to Rockne, and Rice's account of Rockne telling the Gipp story before the 1928 game. Those versions became the basis for the famous Hollywood tale.

However, as Sperber's research later showed, the Rockne and Rice versions were likely fantastical embellishments. In particular, Rice's "confirmation" of having heard of the Gipp request from Rockne before the 1928 game—the only known account ever made—was proven definitively false, as it relied on an alleged meeting between Rice and Rockne that could never have occurred. While Rice claimed this discussion transpired with Rockne in a New York hotel the night before the Army game, contemporary news accounts showed that Rice was nowhere near New York at that time. In fact, he was on site reporting a different football game in the state of Georgia.

It is very possible, perhaps even likely, that Rockne used some version of an embellished Gipp story to fire up the troops that day, but the idea that his words turned the tide don't stand up to scrutiny. For starters, the Irish were not trailing at halftime; the game was a scoreless tie. Throughout the second half, the two teams traded possessions and fought to a 6-6 tie. It was in the game's final minutes that Neimec finally emerged as one of the genuine heroes of the contest.

With time in the game running short, facing a third down and 26 yards to go, and the end-zone nearly half a field away, Neimec took the snap and faded way back to give his receivers time to run downfield. Then, he let loose with a near-perfect pass into the arms of Johnny "One-Play" O'Brien at the Army goal line. O'Brien fell over the line, broke the tie, and promptly headed back to the Notre Dame bench, where Rockne greeted him with a rare embrace.

There was still some drama to play out. The ultimate end of the game was controversial, as the final whistle blew just as Army made a crucial first down at the one-foot yard of Notre Dame and was by rule entitled to one more, potentially victory-clenching, play. The referee who blew the whistle, ending the game, was none other than Walter Eckersall, the famous former football player and later *Chicago Tribune* sports journalist who had been a longtime confidant of Knute Rockne himself.

Twists and turns aside, there were two undeniable facts about the 1928 Notre Dame–Army game. First was that it notched a critical win for Rockne's Ramblers. Second, it demonstrated that Rockne's Boswell, Francis Wallace, had a keen understanding of how important the annual Army–Notre Dame contest was to the ongoing narrative of his alma mater's gridiron team.

GOING INTO THAT 1928 Army game, Notre Dame's season had been at a crossroads. The 4-2 team had already lost games to well-regarded Wisconsin and Georgia Tech and was facing a tough end-of-season matchup against USC. However, a win against Army would extend a two-game winning streak and help set the tone for the end-of-season push.

Having accomplished that critical victory over the Army team, now 5-2, the Irish turned their attention to what would be the final game the program would ever play on tiny Cartier Field. After George Gipp, the Four Horsemen, and Rockne's incredible term as coach—where he had never lost a game on the home field—plans were now underway to play all 1929 home games at Chicago's Soldier Field. As Notre Dame stayed on the road, construction workers would transplant the grass at Cartier Field to the new 54,000-seat Notre Dame Stadium that would open the 1930 season.

The only thing standing between Rockne's perfect home record at Cartier Field and the end-of-season matchup against rival USC was the long-awaited rematch against Wally Steffen, Cyril Letzelter, and the Skibos of Carnegie Tech.

The Rememmatch

The 1926 triumph over Notre Dame represented the end of an astonishing season for Carnegie Tech and Cyril Letzelter. He was the top scorer and top yard gainer of the biggest win in the program's history. Even more, his performance that season not only saw him listed as the second highest scorer on the Tech team, behind senior Bill Donohue, but he was also one of the top twenty-five collegiate scorers on the East Coast with 46 points.

The 1927 season saw Cyril pick up this pace considerably. In the first two games of the season, he scored two touchdowns apiece, and he only failed to cross the goal line in two of Carnegie's ten games.

By the end of the season, he was not only the top scorer for Tech, but his 65 total points scored earned him a rank in the top 15 on the East Coast. His contributions that year represented a third of the total Skibo offense. Over his two varsity seasons, he had proven himself to be an offensive and defensive threat, capable of punishing short game running and speedy open game elusiveness, and a credible receiving threat out of the backfield.

Without a doubt, Letzelter was justified to feel that his star was on the rise as he approached his final season for the Skibos. Like any senior star, he certainly would have felt that the coming season would be his best opportunity yet to shine, and with an increasingly competitive Carnegie Tech program, he like many others judged that the 1928 season held the promise of being an extraordinary year.

Such expectations are what made what happened to Cyril in 1928 so surprising.

The two previous years of success ushered in by stars like Harpster and Letzelter had put Carnegie Tech firmly on the map. And for the first time, the Tartans could be said to have an overabundance of talent, particularly in the backfield. In particular, one of the newest members of the varsity team was one John Karcis, a remarkably talented 220-pound fullback who outweighed Cyril by roughly 30 pounds.

While the preseason chatter clearly had Letzelter ahead of Karcis on the depth chart, after the first spring practice, questions began to arise regarding backfield roles. It was apparent that Karcis was a talent that would be difficult to keep off the field.

Coach Wally Steffen disavowed all preseason talk of converting Letzelter into a blocking back. However, the coaching dynamics at Tech were beginning to change. Not long after the 1926 Notre Dame contest, Steffen began signaling a desire to step away from coaching, noting that the strain of serving as a full-time judge in Illinois and a part-time coach in Pennsylvania was becoming harder to bear each passing year. By the beginning of the 1928 season, Steffen's principal assistant on the ground in Pittsburgh, Bob Waddell, was assuming a greater leadership role. In some news accounts, he was referred to as the head coach, while Steffen became the advisory coach. Steffen was still present at all the games and was still the ultimate authority, but Waddell was assuming a bigger role than he had in the past.

Reviewing how the season played out, it also appears that the coaches focused on increasing the emphasis on the forward pass to take advantage of the skilled senior quarterback, Howard Harpster, and embracing the young, new backfield talent, John Karcis.

On the eve of the season, the coaching staff's intended game plan was for Karcis to take Letzelter's position at fullback. Cyril would still play every down, but he would alternate between fullback and halfback. The result of this new game plan meant that Cyril would have to take on a

Senior Cyril Letzelter applies a block at the legs of a defender while Sophomore John Karcis carries the ball for Carnegie Tech in a 1928 game — a scenario that repeated itself regularly throughout the season, and limited Cyril's offensive output

different role in his senior season. His new responsibilities would put less emphasis on his ball-carrying skills and more emphasis on his backfield blocking, defense, and ability to operate as a backfield receiver.

This change became apparent during the season's very first game against Westminster, where Carnegie ran up a 25-0 lead in the first half, while Cyril, one of the top scorers in the East for two straight seasons, never even touched the ball. By the end of the game, Cyril had been given only six carries, gained 9, and scored an extra point by placekick; all his contributions occurred after the matchup was in the bag.

This pattern would repeat itself week after week. While Harpster threw the ball more than ever, and Karcis took over the primary job of advancing the ball on the ground, Letzelter settled in to make his contributions by throwing blocks for the underclassman and trying to break up the opponent's rhythm while playing defense.

Playing only an eight-game schedule in 1928, through the six games leading up to the contest in South Bend, Letzelter touched the ball only 27 times, an average of under five times per game, and almost always in the second half when the game was usually well in hand. Given what his expectations must have been going into the season, his frustration had to be palpable.

UNLIKE THE 1926 meeting, this time against Notre Dame, Carnegie Tech would be taking no one by surprise. Rockne, for starters, had no intention of skipping the 1928 contest with Carnegie Tech as he had before. He undoubtedly still felt the sting as nary an article discussing the game as it approached failed to mention his having skipped the embarrassing 1926 contest. Also, Rockne had home-field advantage at a location where his team had come away victorious in every game for 22 consecutive years. Outside of Rockne, who characteristically underplayed his team's chances in the media, sportswriters and oddsmakers were still projecting a Notre Dame win. This time, though, they did hedge their bets. Instead of saying a Notre Dame loss was impossible, the oddsmakers on the eve of the game had Notre Dame favored to win by seven points.

Unlike the season to date, there would be one important difference on the Carnegie Tech sideline. For this rematch,

"Advisory Coach" Wally Steffen, who had taken a hands-off approach throughout the season to this point, would be taking a very firm hand. The 1926 game remained the crowning achievement of his program and his coaching career, and he undoubtedly understood that his previous triumph would be rendered a historical fluke if his team were to fall in this rematch, particularly if the primary difference between the contests appeared to be the physical presence of Rockne on the opposing sideline.

Underscoring this point was the fact that every story in advance of the game spoke of the latest battle of wits to be played out between Rockne and Steffen. Regardless of whatever latitude Steffen had given Waddell to run the team to this point, on this day, at Cartier Field, it seems beyond question that Steffen would be calling the shots. Steffen reasserting himself seems even more apparent considering that the Carnegie game plan that day seemed fundamentally different from every other game Tech had played to that point in one crucial respect: it would revolve around the play of one of the heroes of the 1926 game: Cyril Letzelter.

SATURDAY, NOVEMBER 17, 1928, was expected to be a moderate day, at least for late fall. Forecasts had called for clear skies, yet as game time neared, the skies were overcast, and a cold, wet air bit hard through the long coats and hats of the gentlemen, and some ladies, who trod across the muddy grass to the bleachers of Cartier Field.

Built before the turn of the century, Cartier Field bore far more resemblance to a high school track-and-field venue than the home of perhaps the biggest college football program in the country. Situated diagonally and running northwest from approximately the North Gate of where the modern Notre Dame Stadium stands, the location Cartier Field once occupied can be seen on television nearly every home-game Saturday during the fall. Every time the cameras pan from the giant mural of "Touchdown Jesus" on the side of the Theodore M. Hesburgh Library to the reflecting pool on the quadrangle below, one can focus on the left side of that quad and see the piece of earth where George Gipp and the Four Horsemen once ran wild.

Notre Dame's Cartier Field pictured from the sky in late 1922 or early 1923. The famous Administration building with its golden dome and the Basilica of the Sacred Heart provide the backdrop for the north end zone.

The field itself had been christened in 1899 and designed with far more than football in mind. Like many high school venues to this day, the field featured a quarter-mile cinder track around its perimeter and served as the location not just for football but also for baseball and track-and-field events.

Initially, two very basic sets of bleachers stretched along the sidelines for those lucky enough to get a seat. The rest of the crowd would make do, crowding in the open spaces around either end zone, outside the eight-foot gate.

Later modifications in the 1920s would extend the existing bleachers and add additional seating around one of the end zones, creating a horseshoe shape. But it was abundantly clear to all that Cartier Field was no longer adequate to the needs of the Notre Dame football program. As construction of a new stadium would make Cartier Field inaccessible, the following year's 1929 home season would see the Irish call Chicago's Soldier Field home.

But on that cold November day in 1928, there was still one final game to play. And Rockne, whose eleven bore the stain of a stinging defeat against the Skibo crew two years prior, was playing for more than just revenge. He was also trying to protect the legacy of his team's home field, one last time.

DESPITE THE DREARY weather, the air filled with excitement and celebration. The sounds of the marching bands reached the ears of the spectators as they slowly worked their way from the outskirts of the field—where those with automobiles parked in the muddy grass—into the stands, and as the teams took to the field. As promised, Rockne was present, stalking his sideline wearing a long coat and his trademark fedora while his team sat behind him on the grass.

Harpster, the Skibo captain, won the opening toss and elected to defend the north goal, behind which one could easily see the golden dome of the Administration building and the towering steeple of the Basilica of the Sacred Heart. The Irish elected to kick off to start the game.

The Tartans set the tone on the second play when Harpster completed a 58-yard pass, setting his team up on the Notre Dame 12-yard line. On the next play, the call was to Letzelter—it was the first time his number was called during the first quarter the whole season.

He did not disappoint. Upon taking the handoff from Harpster, he barreled through the Notre Dame line for a 12-yard touchdown—his first goal of the season. With Cyril no longer responsible for kicking the extra points, that responsibility fell to Harpster. The Irish blocked the point-after attempt, and the score was Carnegie Tech 6, Notre Dame 0.

Despite the shockingly fast start, Johnny Neimec, the hero of the previous week against Army, no doubt took the field with confidence and fielded Harpster's kickoff ably with a 10-yard return to the Notre Dame 20-yard line. His confidence, however, was shaken when he dropped back to pass on his first play and saw his toss intercepted by Tech on his own 34-yard line. Just like that, the Skibos were already threatening to score again.

This time, the attack was more balanced. Four different Skibo players touched the ball, a pattern more reminiscent of Steffen's game plan two years before. Cyril carried the ball once for a 6-yard gain on the drive, Karcis moved three times for a total of 8 yards, while Howard Eyth and Ted Rosenzweig accounted for the rest. On the seventh play of the drive, Harpster put the ball across on a quarterback sneak and added the extra point as well.

The spectators were still working toward their seats, and Notre Dame was already down 13 points. This start was not Rockne's plan.

AFTER THIS INITIAL flurry of activity, the contest settled into a defensive struggle, with each side rebuffing the other, first downs hard to come by, and the punting game taking center stage. Cyril touched the ball only one more time in the first quarter, the final play, when he burst through the right tackle for a long, 25-yard gain to the Notre Dame 30. His first quarter statistical line was four carries for 43 yards and a touchdown—his average was an eye-opening 10-plus yards per carry.

Ted Rosenzweig got the call on the very next play, at the start of the second quarter, and broke around the end for a 30-yard touchdown. The extra point extended the lead to 20 and ended the suspense about the game's outcome. Unlike 1926, when the play on the gridiron seemed so improbable that many believed the tide would turn almost to the end, in this case it was evident: the boys from Pittsburgh outmatched Rockne's team. Barring a Carnegie collapse, the home-field winning streak would fall, and revenge for 1926 would have to wait for another year.

Nevertheless, three quarters remained, and with the remaining time, Letzelter made the most of every opportunity to remind the assembled throng that, despite his diminished offensive role this season, his gridiron skills remained as sharp as ever.

During the second quarter, Cyril handled the ball four more times, gaining 20 more yards on the ground. The teams went to halftime with Carnegie Tech in command 20-0. When they returned to the field, the Carnegie game plan was simple—hold the ball and keep the lead. They stumbled right out of the gate.

On only the second play of the second half, Harpster fumbled the ball deep in Carnegie Tech territory. The Irish picked up the ball on the Tech 10 and ran the ball in for their first touchdown of the day. Along with the successful extra point, Notre Dame broke the shutout, and the score was 20-7.

On the very next possession, Tech constructed a seven-play drive that drove past midfield into Notre Dame territory. However, facing third and two just over midfield, Ted Rosenzweig took a handoff, advanced 10 yards, and then fumbled the ball. Rockne's eleven recovered at their 35-yard line, having forced their second straight turnover. As quickly as the game had gotten away from Notre Dame at the beginning of the first half, it was coming back into reach as the second half began.

John Neimec and Jack Chevigny worked in tandem over the next nine plays to drive their team almost 40 yards to the Carnegie Tech 29-yard line, and they appeared well on their way to putting additional points on the board. However, their momentum stalled there as Tech stuffed four consecutive attempts to gain yardage. A running play and two attempted passes by Neimec failed to yield a single yard, and Notre Dame's would-be scoring drive ended when they turned over on downs.

Harpster and Karcis were unable to get Tech in gear on the next possession, being forced to punt after three plays failed to move the ball. Fortunately, the Carnegie defense also held strong, and the game once again settled into a long defensive struggle. It wasn't until midway through the fourth quarter that either team was able to earn a first down. During this entire stretch of play, Letzelter inexplicably disappeared again from the offensive game plan, despite the fact that he had been seemingly moving the ball at will every time his number was called all day.

Late in the fourth quarter, Cyril reemerged. After another Carnegie Tech fumble had derailed another potential scoring drive deep in Notre Dame territory, the Skibo defense managed to hold fast and force a punt, which Tech received near midfield. Rather than continue to focus solely on Karcis and Harpster, Letzelter got the first carry of the possession for a two-yard gain. Tech then rotated the ball through all of their playmakers, constructing an eight-play drive that took Tech to the Notre Dame 23-yard line.

Cyril eluding the Notre Dame defense at Cartier Field in 1928, where he scored 2 touchdowns and averaged over 6 yards of offense every time he touched the ball

After Harpster had handed off to Karcis on two straight plays, Tech was faced another third down with seven yards to go. After the snap, Harpster dropped back and flipped a short pass to Letzelter just past the line of scrimmage. Cyril made the most of the opportunity, darting through the Notre Dame secondary and creating a 23-yard touchdown reception. It was his second score of the contest, and the only points Tech scored in the second half. In both scoring plays, he had practically willed his way to the goal line via long runs through the heart of the Notre Dame defense. His efforts extended the score to Carnegie Tech 27, Notre Dame 7.

Despite a furious offensive drive by Notre Dame on the next possession, where they pushed the ball as close as the Carnegie Tech 1-yard line after six short plays; Letzelter's second touchdown essentially iced the game. Their defense came through with an interception to prevent another Notre Dame score, but even if the drive had been successful, there was only time for two more plays before the game clock expired.

The final line of the game for Cyril, especially considering his diminished role on offense, was remarkable. He had scored two touchdowns, one on a running play, and one as a receiver. Though he had only handled the ball on 15 offensive plays, he posted three runs of 10 yards or more. Factoring in his 23-yard touchdown reception, he accounted for 97 total yards. The man who had replaced him in the offense, John Karcis, handled the ball ten more times than Cyril but only accounted for 75 yards and no points. Karcis had also coughed up a critical fumble deep in Notre Dame territory, costing Tech at least three points.

In fact, Cyril's steady play helped obscure the fact that the Tech offense had been incredibly sloppy. They turned the ball over a whopping five times that afternoon. Harpster, Rosenzweig, Flanagan, and Karcis all fumbled, and Harpster also added an interception for good measure. Even Rockne, in later correspondence, lamented his team's inability to take advantage of a myriad of Tech mistakes to make a real game of the contest.

Among the Carnegie backfield players, only Cyril kept the ball safe that day.

It was perhaps for this reason that after the game Coach Steffen proudly awarded the game ball to Letzelter. His play had kept Tech undefeated and positioned them to make a claim for the national championship the following week if they could beat New York University.

Cyril was no doubt proud of this accomplishment, but it also had to be cold comfort. He had been pushed aside all season despite years of elite performance and commitment. He at least could take comfort in the fact that, when given the opportunity, he still produced elite results.

THE FOLLOWING WEEK, the Carnegie eleven found themselves in a position completely foreign. Heading into the final game of the season, they were undefeated, and the eyes of the nation were upon them. The pregame write up by the Associated Press put it best:

> *Like water in a boiler gauge, blood pressures rose all over Pittsburgh tonight as the rabid devotees of king football gathered to predict with appropriate gestures, what would happen tomorrow when the power and punch of New York University collided with the hitherto unstoppable speed and versatility of Carnegie Tech's warriors.*

> *In hotel lobbies and on street corners, knots of pigskin worshippers fought out the battle that two of the greatest teams in the East—and possibly the nation—will wage before 40,000 spectators on Forbes Field. In the balance*

hung an invitation to compete against the cream of the West in the annual tournament of Roses game at Pasadena, Cal. . . . The preponderance of arm-swinging and the sentiment of the general public was reflected in the wagering which made the Skibos of Carnegie a 10-7 favorite.

In three short seasons, Carnegie had grown from an also-ran to a program on the cusp of a national championship. Due chiefly to the strength of their two improbable wins over Rockne's Notre Dame, they were considered one of the best teams in the nation. According to news reports, they already held a provisional invitation from the organizers of the Rose Bowl. All they needed to do was clinch an undefeated record.

New York University, however, was no slouch. They came into the game with only one blemish on their record, having fallen to Georgetown. Not only did they field a perennially strong program, but they also consistently had Carnegie Tech's number. Despite their other successes, Tech had fallen badly to the Violets of New York in 1926 and 1927 during matches in Yankee Stadium. The slight edge from the oddsmakers undoubtedly owed much to the fact that, in this contest, not only was this arguably the strongest team yet in Tech history, but they had the added advantage of playing at home in Pittsburgh.

The city came out in droves to support Tech. Of the estimated 40,000 spectators in attendance, only 2,500 were there to root for New York. Sequestered to a few small sections of the looming ballpark, they arrived with high hopes and low expectations. What they saw was a physical matchup of high intensity and rare levels of brutality. The Pittsburgh Press writeup the following day noted that the tackling in the game "had been the most vicious seen here this season." The first player to be knocked unconscious fell early in the first quarter, on the fourth possession of the game. He would not be the last.

Fresh off his performance of the prior week, Cyril was undoubtedly pleased to figure larger in the offensive game plan than he had most of the season. He was the first player to touch the ball when he received the opening kickoff at his 3-yard line and promptly returned it 18 yards to the Carnegie Tech 21. He only had to wait two plays for his number to be called again, only this time, it was as a receiver. On third down with 2 yards to go, Harpster called for a pass and badly overthrew Letzelter—the ball was uncatchable. The emphasis on the pass and Harpster's inaccuracy with the throw were ominous. After their shaky start, Tech punted away without achieving a first down.

New York University appeared to have a case of the butterflies as well. The team was led by quarterback Ken Strong, who came into the contest as the highest-scoring back in the country, but he got off to an inauspicious start. He threw an incomplete pass, was sacked for 7 yards, and then shanked his first punt for an anemic 18 yards to round out the first Violet possession.

Both teams seemed to struggle throughout the first quarter, with Carnegie struggling to advance the ball and New York fighting to protect it. On his second possession, Strong threw a critical interception to Harpster, which led to the first sustained drive of the day by Carnegie, with Tech marching almost 40 yards before being forced to punt. Harpster's effort produced a touchback, so Strong and NYU took possession

192

again at their own 20. After their own solid effort, including 30 yards of offense by Strong alone, he threw another interception to Harpster.

Tech wasted no time capitalizing on the error, with Harpster immediately connecting on a first-down pass to Anthony Sweet for a 45-yard touchdown. Cyril added the extra point, and the favored Skibos staked a 7-0 lead.

Despite the early lead, however, the play on the field was telling another story. New York's Ken Strong was obviously playing on another level compared to the other 21 men on the field. Immediately after Tech scored, Strong executed a 15-yard completion and a 26-yard run on consecutive plays to drive quickly into Carnegie territory. Unlike almost anyone Tech had faced to this point, he seemed capable of moving the ball at will by ground or through the air. The only factor slowing New York down was either penalties or their own mistakes, and as the game wore on, the mistakes were gradually corrected.

It was a critical drive late in the second quarter that turned the tide against the Skibos. Using their full complement of backfield talent, Strong directed the Violets quickly downfield with one major play after another. At one point, when the NYU halfback broke free for a 36-yard run, it was only Letzelter's sprinting tackle from behind that saved Tech from suffering a game-tying touchdown. But the reprieve was short-lived. Three more plays of more than 15 years combined to put the Violets on the board. At the break, it was a tie score, but it was apparent that Tech would need to elevate its play to survive the second half.

As it was, Carnegie never found its stride and ran a playbook that was at times overly cautious, with repeated punting on early downs, and needlessly aggressive, with a greater emphasis on passing than had been previously seen by the Skibos. Harpster, for his part, was uncharacteristically inaccurate in his passing, repeatedly making throws that were reportedly uncatchable. It was as if Tech couldn't even settle on a game plan.

By all accounts, the play on the field remained ferocious through all four quarters of the contest. In the fourth quarter alone, Carnegie hit Ken Strong so hard on a tackle that he lost consciousness—although he recovered and stayed in the game. Later that same quarter, Tech took down NYU captain and lineman Al Lassman so viciously that a stretcher was requested to remove him from the arena. The teams later learned he suffered a skull fracture. Lack of intensity in facing this must-win game was clearly not an issue for the Carnegie eleven.

And yet it wasn't enough. In the end, New York had the better team, and in Strong, they had the best playmaker on the field. It showed as they controlled the second half and eventually won 27-13.

For his part, Cyril delivered a solid if unspectacular performance. He was used out of the backfield mostly as a receiver, where he notched several impressive receptions and contributed with some short-yardage runs. His biggest contributions were on special teams, where his kick returns consistently impressed. But, despite the fact that Cyril became a significant part of the offensive game plan during the season's final two games, he had to feel deep disappointment at coming so close to a championship yet falling short.

Even so, Cyril's all-around play was recognized enough to gain him national acclaim, as he ended up as a runner-up for the 1928 version of the All-American Team annually selected by Tad Jones, Pop Warner, and Knute Rockne. Nevertheless, he also watched as his teammate Harpster made the first team. Ironically, this was the same group of men that met together to name the 1926 team two years prior while they attended the Army-Navy game in Chicago, as Cyril, Harpster, and Carnegie Tech were dealing Notre Dame that humiliating 1926 defeat at Forbes Field.

Of his three seasons at Carnegie Tech, his final year was one where Cyril demonstrated his commitment to the team when he stepped back from the spotlight to make room for the younger stars. Though it was arguably the right thing for the team, there was undoubtedly some disappointment.

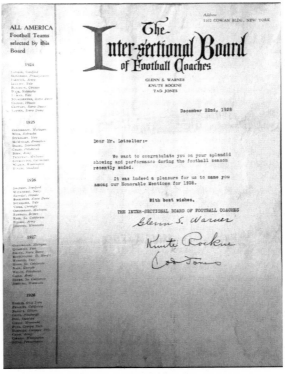

The letter sent to Cyril by "Pop" Warner, Knute Rockne and Tad Jones naming him a runner-up to the 1928 All-American Team, despite his reduced role on offense that season

That, probably more than anything, was why Cyril wasted little time in trying to find a way to extend his football life. It was no surprise that when he began searching for answers to the next phase of his life, his longtime mentor, J. F. Mullaney, already had a plan.

In the Army Now

At the close of Cyril's senior season, he received one final accolade. Along with teammates Howard Harpster and Anthony Sweet, he was named to the All-East team and earned a trip to a new annual event launched only three years prior: the East-West Shrine game in San Francisco, California. As one of only 28 players from the East to be named, the recognition cemented the fact that, despite his diminished offensive role that season, Cyril remained among the elite backfield players the country had to offer.

If they hadn't begun already, it seems a fair assumption that Cyril's discussions over what to do next began in earnest shortly after that trip to California. How he arrived at his ultimate decision is a matter of speculation, except for the fact that Bud Mullaney played an essential role in plotting his next step.

What is certain is that in a matter of weeks, by March of 1929, Mullaney was already leveraging his considerable network and contacts to help secure Cyril an appointment to the only place in America where he could extend his football career: the United States Military Academy at West Point.

Coincidentally, it was during the same period that Mullaney was laying his plans to continue Cyril's playing career with a military appointment that Congressman Hamilton Fish was beginning to wage his war against the Point over his view that the academy's ability to field college graduates on the gridiron constituted an unfair competitive advantage. It was in this sense that Cyril's efforts to gain

197

admission, although unknown at the time, helped prove Fish's point. Even Cyril's half sister, Betty Hamm, made it clear many decades later, in a 2013 interview, that the efforts undertaken on Cyril's behalf were completely in service of his desire to continue playing football.

So Mullaney went to work, as fixers do, to make the necessary arrangements. But unlike leveraging his relationships to get Cyril into Carnegie Tech, securing him a place in West Point was no easy trick. To this day, few institutions in the United States are more exclusive than the United States Military Academy.

WEST POINT SITS on a plateau on the western bank of the Hudson River, a tactically important position during the Revolutionary War. According to historians at the academy, then-General George Washington considered the location so advantageous that he thought it the most important strategic position in America. It was at Washington's direction that the construction of the forts and artillery batteries that make up the academy began.

From its earliest days as a military academy, an appointment to West Point was a highly coveted prize. Not just anyone could attend the military academy. The process involved in obtaining a place as a cadet seems designed to achieve two specific goals: First, the requirement of candidates to pass extremely rigorous entrance exams ensured that cadets would have the requisite academic chops to lead the nation's military. Second, the requirement that exclusive political leaders first nominate candidates limited access to the academy to those capable of gaining the attention and favor of existing political elites. In a sense, showing the smarts and savvy necessary to win admission to the academy was in itself a test as to whether a potential cadet had what it took to make it at West Point.

Since its inception, the process of gaining an appointment to West Point has remained largely unchanged. A candidate must be nominated either by a member of the United States Congress or by the vice president or president of the United States, and the number of nominations a member of Congress can make is strictly limited. While the number has ebbed and flowed over time based on the approved enrollment for the academy, in general members of Congress are not allowed to have more than five nominees attending the academy at any time. In more simple terms, a member of Congress can make roughly one nomination per year.

In searching for a path into West Point for Cyril, Mullaney turned his gaze to the incumbent congressman from Steubenville, Ohio, Benjamin Franklin Murphy. Frank, as he was known, was first elected to Congress in 1918, just a few years after the death of Cyril's mother. Initially a glassworker by trade, he dabbled later in a variety of businesses, including real estate and banking. He eventually served as the vice president of the People's National Bank until the Great War, when he served at Camp Sheridan in Montgomery, Alabama.

By the time Mullaney came calling, Murphy had been in Congress for a decade, and it is fair to assume that by that point, the representative had relationships with his home communities' most significant employers. None loomed larger than the local steel plants operated by Wheeling Steel—the same Wheeling Steel that operated the Yorkville Tin Mill managed by Mullaney, and that had employed Cyril over the summers since he had graduated from high school.

The Wheeling Steel Plant in Steubenville was a remarkable sight to behold. Stretching over a mile in length along the river, it was one of the largest plants of its kind in the entire Ohio Valley. The plant produced a wide variety of steel products and boasted two blast furnaces, eleven open hearth mills, and a hot strip mill. River vessels owned by the company dominated the waterway, and the company maintained its own private railroad tracks on the site. Its presence as a lynchpin of the local economy was apparent, and local elected officials were undoubtedly well acquainted with the industry and the executives who ran the show.

There is little doubt that Mullaney's status as patent-holding steel mill administrator with Wheeling Steel would have made it very easy for him to open communications with Murphy's congressional office. How the conversation between the two parties began is unknown. What is known, however, is that Cyril was high enough on the congressman's radar that he gained admittance to the official entrance examination conducted during the first week of March 1929. Further, by the second week of April, it was clear that Cyril had at least cleared the academic hurdle because Mullaney now appeared confident he had secured a commitment from Murphy to appoint Cyril to the academy. We know this because of the correspondence that still exists from the period between Cyril and Mullaney.

Specifically, on April 17, 1929, Mullaney sent a hand-written letter to Cyril in Pittsburgh letting him know that he had been in close communication with Murphy's congressional staff and that he had been directed to have Cyril send a personalized letter to the congressman requesting the appointment. Leaving nothing to chance, Mullaney gave his protégé very specific instructions, including that use a typewriter and compose the note on Carnegie Tech letterhead. Mullaney also provided a complete, handwritten version of the letter that Cyril was to have typewritten and sent directly to Congressman Murphy.

Cyril must have acted on Mullaney's instructions immediately, because exactly two weeks later, on the afternoon of May 1, 1929, Congressman Murphy ordered Western Union to send a telegram to its office in Pittsburgh, earmarked for Cyril Letzelter. It read simply:

> *HAVE THIS DAY RECOMMENDED YOUR APPOINTMENT AS A CADET TO WESTPOINT MY HEARTY GOOD WISHES GO TO YOU WITH THIS MESSAGE*
>
> *FRANK MURPHY*

A recommendation was not an appointment—not yet at least. Official word would have to wait another eight weeks, until Cyril received a second telegram, this time from Major General Charles Higbee Bridges, the adjutant general of the United States Army, reading:

> *LETTER MAILED AUTHORIZING YOU TO REPORT TO SUPERINTENDENT AT WEST POINT NY ON JULY FIRST FOR ADMISSION AS CADET*
>
> *BRIDGES*

Any impression that Cyril was headed to West Point for any reason other than football was quickly allayed by the fact that Letzelter's appointment was front-page news on sports pages across the country. Nearly every story not only emphasized his addition to the football team but featured the same angle—that the arrival of Cyril at the academy spelled bad news for Knute Rockne and the Notre Dame eleven. One especially overwrought passage read:

> *Knute Rockne never has any luck. Just when it began to look as though the Carnegie Tech jinx had been shaken off, Knute will wake up today to learn that his game with the Army this year be just another of those "damn Carnegie Tech things."*

> *An important cog in those two crushing defeats handed Rockne in the last three years, Cyril Letzelter, the rugged halfback, will be graduated just in time at Carnegie Tech to accept the scholarship offered him by Congressman Frank Murphy of the eighteenth Ohio district, to enter West Point and be a football candidate this fall.*

If the sports pages across the country took note, we should assume Rockne himself did as well. While it is not clear if he acted at Rockne's direction, we do know for certain that Francis Wallace took very special note of the appointment—because not long after, Wallace himself returned to the valley he once called home and started asking uncomfortable questions about Cyril Letzelter of Martins Ferry.

MEANWHILE, CONGRESSMAN HAMILTON Fish continued his quixotic efforts to combat the West Point football eligibility guidelines, to little effect. Having recently failed in his efforts to pressure Secretary of War Good to impose a solution on the impasse between the Naval and Army academies, Fish joined forces with Congressman Fred Britten—the chairman of the House Armed Services Committee—in personally enlisting the assistance of none other than President Herbert Hoover.

In a news release on June 10, 1929, Britten expressed his intent to take the issue to the president "if other means prove unsuccessful." The release was a barely veiled threat to the academies to make a deal before the powerful chairman went over their heads. While Britten and Fish acknowledged that Secretary Good had chosen not to embrace the plan offered previously by Fish for a compromise, it was clear that both congressmen favored imposing the four-year eligibility rule onto West Point from above, and they made clear their intent to make such an outcome their priority. The threats, however, fell on deaf ears, and the issue itself dropped from view until later that fall when Fish saw an opportunity to actually raise the profile of the issue with Hoover.

According to a *New York Times* report, on September 25th of that year, Fish personally requested the president intervene with the secretaries of war and navy, the superintendents of both Annapolis and West Point, and their respective athletic directors. Specifically, he requested the president to force them to convene, work out their differences, and resume the traditional football rivalry. Of course, right after his discussion, Fish made a beeline to the media, announcing that Hoover had been receptive to his suggestion, while at the same time threatening that failure to break the impasse could lead to Congressional remedies. Fish was careful not to wade too far into the issue of eligibility, keeping his focus on the resumption of the rivalry.

However, there is little evidence that Hoover did more than pay lip service to Fish's request. While a few weeks later, Hoover did issue a statement suggesting he wanted the series to resume, there are no indications that the summit of military secretaries and academy superintendents actually convened to discuss the matter. And there was clearly no effort to address the player eligibility issue at the heart of the dispute.

If anything, Hoover's only tepid endorsement of resuming the series appeared to embolden West Point. A week after his remarks, representatives of the Navy made it clear that they were willing to meet Army in a postseason contest without preconditions on player eligibility. Even so, Army demurred, stating that the only possible date for postseason play— suggested as December 6—was in conflict with the end-of-term examinations at West Point. There would be no game in 1929. Adding insult to injury, Superintendent William Smith was publicly unwavering in the position that West Point would not be changing its eligibility guidelines for any future contests.

While Fish had succeeded in getting plenty of press coverage, he had utterly failed in making real progress on either changing the West Point eligibility guidelines or in moving the academies toward a resumption of their football rivalry. Making his case on the merits alone wasn't gaining enough traction to move the ball, so to speak. What Fish needed was something extra to help construct his argument.

Enter Christian Cagle.

IF HAMILTON FISH was ever looking for a perfect example of what he was railing against at West Point, he needed to look no further than Christian "Red" Cagle. Cagle arrived at the military academy in 1926 as a genuine football star, not unlike how Cyril would appear three years later in 1929.

Before arriving at West Point, Cagle was a highly talented tailback for Southwestern Louisiana Institute from 1923 to 1925, where he set the school's career scoring record on the strength of 10 kickoff returns for touchdowns. A multi-tool player, he was a superb passer, averaged over 10 yards per carry when rushing, and converted 20 of 25 dropkick scoring attempts during his time in Louisiana. It was said that he had thighs "as big as watermelons" that helped account for his tremendous speed and ability to change direction on the gridiron.

Playing varsity for West Point, he was the first player ever to be named to Grantland Rice's All-American Team for three consecutive years, in 1927, 1928, and 1929. His senior year with Army, before the era of Heisman Trophy, he was named College Football Player of the Year.

Clearly, Cagle was a highly talented player who came to the academy with extensive collegiate experience. But this wasn't what drew him to Fish's attention. It was how Cagle ended his career at West Point that rocked the sports world and gave Fish fresh fuel for his ongoing feud with the Army program.

On May 9, 1930, Cagle dropped an unexpected bomb on the sporting world by announcing that, immediately upon his graduation, he would be resigning his commission in the officer corps. The justification he gave was jarring:

> *It is with considerable regret that I shall submit my resignation to the War Department after graduation in order to accept two positions in civil life, one as football coach at Mississippi A & M, and the other with a large commercial house. The combined salary is considerably more than the pay of a Major General, a rank I would indeed be most fortunate to attain after thirty or thirty-five years of service.*

Cagle went on in his statement to lament that the pay for a second lieutenant would require that he live in a state of "genteel poverty." He further hinted that the prospect of successfully enacting legislation pending before the Congress to raise officer pay—legislation that had no chance of passage—might have caused him to reconsider. As it was, he was only bowing to political and economic realities.

As stunning as Cagle's announcement was, what made it more remarkable was the fact that the academy had allowed Cagle to make any statement at all. The ethos of the academy was such that the institution went great lengths to eliminate any appearance of favoritism within the cadet ranks. All cadets were delivered a consistent message that they would all graduate from the academy equally as second lieutenants and that their military careers would be evaluated on merit.

Not only did allowing Cagle to make the announcement defy that standard, but by making the release before completion of his final exams or his actual graduation, Cagle was being allowed to resign publicly a commission he had not yet earned. Despite the fact that the superintendent of the academy, Major General William R. Smith, said he made the special exception allowing Cagle to make the announcement "because of the public's interest in this young man"—unmistakably referring to the cadet's renown on the gridiron—the whole episode invited controversy and scrutiny.

In retrospect, it appears that Smith was using Cagle's decision to lobby on behalf of the doomed pay bill before the Congress. Smith even noted in his public statement about his cadet, "I am informed that of the last five classes of cadets graduated here at least forty-four have resigned soon after graduation, the majority for financial reasons. This means that the nation lost a number of young officers of great value."

However, Smith's apparent intent to use the Cagle resignation in this fashion blew up spectacularly in his face just four days later. The controversy exploded when the Associated Press confronted West Point with official court records showing that Cagle had secretly married during a furlough in August of 1928—almost two years previously—in a clear violation of the West Point honor code. Additional contemporary reports recently uncovered also show that Cagle had accepted his coaching position with Mississippi A&M in April, over a month before he announced his intent to resign his position. In short, Cagle married secretly almost two years prior and then proceeded to complete his junior and senior seasons on the Army gridiron. Over that period, he simultaneously plotted an exit from his military obligations. The totality of the evidence begged the question: did Cagle ever intend to accept his commission, or was it all a charade?

The academy appears to have been completely blindsided by the new information. Confronted with the evidence, Smith immediately went into damage control mode. He urgently asked for and received Cagle's immediate resignation. But this was, of course, purely cosmetic. Cagle had already effectively resigned and was pointed toward a more lucrative career in both business and professional football. For West Point, the damage was already done.

Hamilton Fish, as one could imagine, wasted no time capitalizing on this fresh blood in the water. Two days after the news of Cagle's forbidden marriage broke, he took to the floor of the House of Representatives and hijacked a routine debate over appropriations for the Naval Academy. Changing the subject, Fish proceeded to thunder against the recent events at West Point and tie the Cagle scandal into his broader agenda against the player eligibility guidelines for the Army football team.

For twenty minutes Fish, with help from his colleague Congressman Britten and several other friendly questioners, spoke in the peculiar, gentlemanly tones reserved for members of the United States Congress. Together, they proceeded to savage West Point on every major issue Fish had raised over the preceding 18 months and even went so far as to discuss whether the option of a court-martial of Cagle was possible.

On the Cagle matter, there was no question that Fish and his allies were on very solid ground. Fish opened his remarks by quickly recounting the remarkable events of the previous week, and then reasonably suggested that an investigation was warranted to determine if any officers at West Point were aware that Cagle had been married for nearly two years while attending the military academy.

Had Fish kept his remarks focused on the Cagle affair, he might have had more success. As it was, Fish's passion got the better of him. He quickly strayed away from the clear facts of the Cagle controversy into more murky questions of West Point's eligibility rules. Unfortunately for his cause, he promptly tripped into hyperbole when describing the situation at West Point, stating, "For the last few years over 50 percent of all the members of the Army football teams have been former college stars."

For the congressman, this was no doubt a throwaway line in a debate to which he likely had given little thought. But Fish was the member of Congress who represented the community of West Point in the House of Representatives, and he was using the floor of the Congress to attack the Army and question the honor of those operating the country's most elite military academy. Already moving into unprecedented territory with his fusillade, Fish needed to be careful in making his case. But his missionary zeal led him to overplay his hand, and it gave the Army the opening they needed to both shift the debate away from the embarrassing Cagle controversy and to undercut Fish's ongoing crusade against West Point football.

Three days later, on May 20, Secretary of War Patrick Hurley ordered his adjutant general to send a letter to Major General H. A. Drum, the inspector general, asking for an immediate investigation in response to the claims leveled by Fish from the House floor. The direction given by Hurley left no doubt about Army's plan, as the requested scope went far beyond anything suggested during the previous day's congressional discussion. Specifically, the asked scope of inquiry read as follows:

1. *It has been alleged:*

    a. That the Army Athletic Association is grafting or stealing money for themselves from the funds of the Association.
    b. That the association has paid scouts traveling, who pick players and establish liaison with Congressmen and secure their appointments to West Point with the distinct understanding that they will be allowed to leave West Point or the Army when they have finished their football associations at the academy.

    c. That funds of the Army Athletic Association are used to pay players at West Point extra compensation.

2. *The Secretary of War directs that the Inspector General investigate personally these charges and examine thoroughly every activity and all methods pursued by the Athletic Association or other agencies with a view to ascertaining the truth or falsity of all or any portion of the allegations.*

3. *It is alleged that 50 per cent of the West Point football teams during the last seven years were college men who had already played three years on the college teams.*

Notably, Chris Cagle's name and the incident surrounding his departure from West Point is not mentioned as the leading purpose of the investigation. Also noteworthy is the fact that the allegations to be investigated read more like a compilation of critiques generally leveled at the Army program since the break in relations with Annapolis and bore little resemblance to the topics discussed by Fish and his colleagues the previous day. The implication was clear. In Fish's intemperate and exaggerated remarks, they saw an opportunity for a counterattack, and they planned to take full advantage.

The particulars and scope of the Army investigation authorized by Secretary Hurley would not be known to rank and file members of Congress for several weeks when the secretary himself released a statement to the media referencing the upcoming report while accusing Fish personally of making false allegations about the Army program. He explicitly noted Fish's "50 percent" accusation and included the charges of financially subsidizing players in stating, "The only grievous thing the matter with these statements by Mr. Fish, is that they are both untrue."

Fish immediately went on the defensive, releasing his own statement noting—correctly—that he had never alleged players were being subsidized, and he accused the secretary of distorting his words. Interestingly, Fish also began to back off the "50 percent" allegation, now stating that the number was "30 to 50 percent" and suggesting that it was an accurate statement when applied to past team captains, and not the team as a whole. Fish, ever indignant, called on Secretary Hurley to issue him an apology.

Not surprisingly, Hurley ignored Fish's initial response, so the congressman then dashed off a formal letter to the secretary protesting Hurley's misrepresentation of his position and challenging Hurley to produce proof he had ever actually claimed Army players were subsidized. Fish even put money on the table, offering to donate $100 to the charity of Hurley's choice if he could produce the evidence.

It does not appear that Hurley ever replied to Fish's challenge. But if Fish thought that settled the matter, he was highly mistaken, because Hurley, the Army, and their supporters weren't done with Fish yet.

A week later, on June 17, with no apparent warning, Congressman Roy Fitzgerald of Ohio, himself an Army veteran of World War I, took to the House floor to reveal the results of the investigation and have the Drum Report entered officially into the Congressional Record. In so doing he also delivered a comprehensive rebuke to Army's critics and leveled a blistering attack on Congressman Fish's integrity.

The crux of Fitzgerald's chief remarks boiled down to two central points. First, the report showed no evidence of the type of corruption suggested by Hurley's letter. This was not surprising, as those charges were already exaggerated for the distinct purpose of proving them wrong. Second, about Fish's allegation that 50 percent of the Army team was made up of previous college stars, it showed how far off the mark this really was.

The report specifically listed all 163 men who had played on the Army football teams since 1923 and detailed the level of their previous involvement in football at other collegiate institutions. The contrast between what Army

212

reported and what Fish had alleged was stark. Only 10 percent of Army players had played so much as one year of college before entering the academy. Only 6 percent had logged three years of football before coming to West Point. Ordinarily, such numbers would have bolstered Fish's case. But because he so wildly exaggerated the facts, what should have been information that helped him was instead used to impeach his credibility.

Having made those points, Fitzgerald then went on to suggest that complaints about the difference in the eligibility standards between West Point and Annapolis were better explained by understanding the statutory differences between the two academies themselves.

Specifically, Fitzgerald eloquently laid out the case that it was a federal law that dictated who was and was not eligible to attend the two academies and pointed out that the law all but guaranteed that the Naval Academy would always have a younger student body. This was because Naval Academy nominees were eligible for admission a full year younger than was the case for West Point. Annapolis also cut off enrollment eligibility a full year before West Point. The result was that historically, going back decades, the Annapolis team always skewed younger. This discrepancy, he pointed out, was built into the law and would require an act of Congress to change.

He further made the case that both academies, as a matter of principle, adopted the stance that all nominees entered their institutions with a blank slate. The curriculum was identical for all, the regulations were identical, and the evaluations were identical. Participants were to rise and fall based on merit and performance, and their lives and experience before entering were deemed irrelevant.

As a result, according to Fitzgerald, the Naval Academy, in complaining about the makeup of teams fielded by Army, were in effect asking to meet on the gridiron only if Army promised to field an inferior squad that was not reflective of the full cadet class. Such a request, according to Fitzgerald, was nothing more than asking to play with a handicap. He stated, "That academy is what it is in accordance with the law, and you either compete with West Point or you are afraid or you do not dare or you do not care to compete with West Point because the men at West Point are, by the law of the United States, stronger, more able, more vigorous, and more virile then the men of some other institution."

As a parting shot, Fitzgerald even suggested that Navy might be better served requesting a contest against the Army's freshman squad, or perhaps even the second team.

Finally, Fitzgerald turned his eye toward Congressman Fish himself.

Noting repeatedly that a cadet could not enter either service academy without a nomination from a member of Congress, the vice president, or the president, Fitzgerald made it clear that the accusations of shenanigans regarding recruitment of cadets for athletic purposes amounted to slurs against members of Congress—a very severe contention. He pointed out that, as the Representative of the very congressional district that hosted West Point, one would have expected Congressman Fish to be one of the institution's greatest champions, not its most prominent critic; and he openly questioned if other, unknown factors might be at play. He

214

closed his stemwinder with Fish directly in the crosshairs, saying,

> Such unfortunate statements as those made on the floor of Congress call for explanations of the lack of information and possibly the source of any passionate hostility to West Point on the part of our distinguished colleague, who should be its sponsor and interpreter to the nation.
>
> If the gentleman is conscious of any patriotic interest in the Military Academy, he will, of course, retract the inaccurate statements that he has made, for otherwise he could well be regarded as an enemy of this great school of our national defense, and many will wonder what animus, what motives, have actuated him.

The next day the *New York Times* ran an exclusive story discussing the findings of the Drum Report and detailing how its conclusions contradicted the "outburst" by Congressman Fish the previous month. Fish was predictably incensed.

Three days later, an unbowed Fish returned to the House floor in an attempt to defend his honor. After first reading the letter he had sent Secretary Hurley the prior week into the record, the congressman from New York proceeded to make a case that his "50 percent" allegation was, in fact, justified. But the qualifications necessary to get the numbers to fit served to further reinforce how much of a stretch his initial comments had been.

To make his case, he used his own methodology that ignored nearly half of the active team roster and counted only the top players who had earned their full varsity letter. Also, he focused specifically on the teams from 1926 to 1928, which seemed an arbitrary choice in that it ignored the most recent Army season and included a season where Army and Navy had not met on the gridiron at all. Finally, he counted any prior college experience, however brief, as sufficient to substantiate his claim that these players qualified as college "stars." Not surprisingly, he suggested that his own methodology indicated as much as 70 percent of recent Army teams were made up of former college stars.

There is little evidence that anyone regarded Fish's efforts with seriousness. Army had effectively undercut the congressman's credibility and produced a fairly comprehensive internal report. That report not only contradicted Fish's claims but used his willingness to take his grievance to the floor of the Congress as a platform for a wide-ranging counterattack on the foes of the Army program and how it operated.

This exchange had been the biggest battle to date in Hamilton Fish's war, and there was little doubt that the Army had won the round convincingly.

CYRIL'S FIRST YEAR at West Point took place in the background of Chris Cagle's senior year at the academy and his tumultuous, high-profile exit. While Letzelter's first year wasn't nearly so high profile, it certainly was turbulent.

Beyond the legends both famous and infamous who have walked its halls, the United States Military Academy at West Point is known for other things, such as its legendary reputation for the hazing of "plebes," or freshmen.

Generally speaking, plebes—often referred to by tradition at the USMA as "Mr. Ducrot" or "Dumbjohn" by the upperclassmen—would work hard to comply with demands so that their would-be tormentors would divert their attention to another poor soul. This made it all the more remarkable that when Letzelter arrived at West Point on July 1, 1929, wearing dark pants, a white button-up shirt worn loosely at the collar, and no tie, he was asked by an upperclassman condescendingly, "What are you famous for, Mr. Ducrot?"

Letzelter, showing uncharacteristic cheek for a plebe, calmly replied, "For making two touchdowns against Notre Dame in one game." It was an answer that left his would-be tormentor momentarily speechless, but perhaps not surprised,

Cyril Letzelter, second from left, arrives at West Point on July 1, 1929 and immediately faces hazing from upperclassmen.

because it was already known that Cy Letzelter went to West Point to continue doing what he did best—play football.

Whatever short-term advantage his prior football exploits earned him upon his arrival, it wasn't long until the great democracy of West Point, which always aimed to level the playing field for all cadets, began to wear him down. According to the accounts of his family and surviving correspondence between Cyril and his father, he had a very challenging time adjusting to his new role as a "plebe."

This is understandable. Whatever the disappointments of his senior season at Carnegie Tech, he had still performed well enough that season to merit an honorable mention on the annual All-American Team and had represented the All-East team in California in the postseason. Also, as the vice president of his senior class, he was a well-respected "big man on campus." Now he had arrived at an institution whose mission combined the use of rigorous academics, punishing physical activity, and sometimes brutal hazing to dramatically pound the independence out of new cadets. To rebuild them into the leaders of tomorrow's military, West Point would first tear each of them down.

Also, despite the role football played in his desire to go to West Point, there would be no varsity football activity in his first year, as Army did honor the same rule as many other institutions that forbade freshmen from playing on varsity teams. The climb down from varsity football hero to lowly plebe was undoubtedly steep.

Nothing demonstrated the difficulties Cyril was having acclimating to West Point more than the surviving letters he received from his own father during that first term. They are the words of a father who knows his son is struggling and is desperately looking for a way to communicate encouragement, faith, and love, and almost willing him to prevail over his challenges. Referring to the difficulties Cyril was facing, he reminded his son this wasn't his first time facing hard times, writing in late September of 1929:

> *You know that your life has not been the most pleasant in the past, but it was never of my choosing. In think many and many times how much pleasanter (sic) and loving home would have been for you if you had had a mother, and how her care and love could awaken the spirit in you that I am hoping to do. I know how proud she would be of you today if she were living, because she was a thoroughbred through and through. I only wish you could have known her as I knew her, because she knew no failure in anything, and I have seen her spirit in you, and know that it is there, but you will have to fight yourself and bring it out. I know you can do it and will not fail.*

At this point, Cyril was just over two months at the academy, and it was already clear that he was struggling greatly with his classwork. The correspondence from his father is enlightening, as it describes how, when it came to his schooling, up to that point, Cyril's mind was perpetually elsewhere. His letters make repeated references to past academic struggles both at Martins Ferry high school and at Carnegie Tech. It becomes apparent that, to this point, Cyril had been a young man who benefitted from both his status as an athlete and his own natural charm to advance through the academic ranks with minimal output. In November 1929, his father wrote him, "When you were in high school you know your grades were not the best and your greatest weakness was to always try and excuse yourself and get through the easiest

219

way. When you went to Tech you had in mind a certain course mapped out, but after the first year, what did you do? The same thing, try to excuse yourself and took the easiest way out."

Despite the fact that football had been the driving force in his decision to go to West Point, unlike his previous educational experiences, the academy did not allow him to cut corners. The reality check appears to have been a quite a shock for Cyril.

Perhaps nothing drove this point home more than the events surrounding what was supposed to be one of the highlights of his first year. As a member of the yearling football team, Cyril would be eligible to take the postseason trip with the entire football program to Palo Alto, California, for a post-Christmas contest at Stanford. They would be traveling by a train specially equipped for the journey. On the afternoon of December 18, the Army cadets arrived at the station in Albany, New York, for the long, transcontinental ride.

In an embarrassing incident that occurred in front of reporters and was included prominently in news coverage of the event, Cyril and another classmate were informed at 2:45, just 15 minutes before their departure, that they had failed their final exams in English and would not be allowed onto the train. As it was reported, "The two saluted, turned on their heels and walked out. But they didn't turn before disappointment crossed their faces. Immediately Bryan issued orders for two men to take their place and the disappointment of Letzelter and O'Reilly provided the joy of Graham and DeGrave."

That previous December, Letzelter had made headlines as a Carnegie Tech senior and member of the All-East team and had traveled to San Francisco to play in the annual East-West game. One year later, on the eve of a similar trip, he instead made headlines as he suffered this very public academic failure. His friends and colleagues boarded their exclusive train with private food and water services, dining cars and drawing cars and sleeper cars, knowing that for the next three weeks, they would all be released from the strict routines of the military academy. For Cyril, he returned to West Point. There would be no rest or break. Instead, he would be expected to work with a tutor, double down on his studies, and bring his grades up in short order.

If he expected sympathy from his father, he wasn't getting any. He soon received a letter from his father that began, "We see by the papers that you did not get to make the trip to the coast with your teammates, and no doubt feel blue about that. Forget it. It is in the past. . . . You know now that you will have to work harder than ever so forget it and make up your mind to do it." His father also slyly added that a some of his Christmas presents from a family friend would be arriving late, as they had been shipped to Palo Alto, where he was expected to be on Christmas.

Unlike his other letters, this one was short on encouragement and more matter-of-fact in its tone. Perhaps because it was the holiday season, his dad also wrote to him about finding solace in his faith. The letter was a brief, powerful example of the application of Catholic guilt. In any event, it made enough of an impression that it was one of only three letters from his father that Cyril apparently kept for the rest of his life. All three had been written during his first months at West Point, and all three had exhorted him to overcome his challenges, grow up, and become a man. They clearly had an important impact, which was a good thing, because Cyril's greatest challenges were yet to come.

The Crash

To his credit, Cyril managed to pull himself together academically during the latter half of his first year as a cadet. The *Pittsburgh Press*, which continued to follow his career closely even after he had left Carnegie Tech, amusingly ran a

story under the headline "Geoffrey Chaucer Kayoed By Punch Drunk Letzelter" reporting that he had successfully brought his grades into line and would be eligible for the fall Army gridiron campaign. It also began to set expectations for Cyril, as he was

Cyril strikes an intimidating pose in a promotional photo used prior to the 1930 Army football season.

reported to be the natural successor to Chris Cagle himself, stating, "Chaucer had Letzelter punch drunk for weeks. Letzelter, you know, is the boy that the Cadets figure as the logical man for 'Rede' (as Chaucer would spell it) Cagle's empty shoes. But Letzelter, after weeks of despair and nightmares in which he was being 'found' has managed to crush the evil English, the subject that had him in dire danger of being dropped from the Academy."

As the season grew nearer, story after story stressed how the new Army coach, Major Ralph Sasse, was building the team around Cyril's talents and pointing toward the all-important match against Notre Dame. The Associated Press reported on Sasse's preseason meetings with none other than "Pop" Warner himself to prepare a game plan for the season that would adopt the Stanford coach's system of wing-back formations and quick-breaking plays, of which Letzelter was to be a pivotal part.

The season got off to a quick start on September 27 against Boston University, with Cyril scoring the team's first points of the year on a short touchdown run not long after Army recovered a fumble deep in opposing territory. He added the extra point as well, staking the team to an early 7-0 lead. Despite the fact that the starters sat for over half the game, Letzelter's play was strong enough to gain widespread praise for his "remarkable power and versatility."

The early glow of promise was short-lived, however, because three days later, the United States Secretary of War received the letter that would ultimately lead to the end of Cyril's Army football career.[1]

---

[1]Reconstructing the events that led to the letter sent to Secretary of War Hurley is difficult, as much of the official record and survivors from the era have been lost to time.

Betty Letzelter Hamm, who was Cyril's half sister by way of Michael Letzelter's second wife, was the only surviving relative from the era with firsthand knowledge of what transpired and how it was viewed by the family. Prior to her death in 2018, she was interviewed in 2013 and in 2014 about the relevant events. The most important insight of hers was that the first inkling of trouble was when, in her words, "There (was) a man, of course he's passed away now. His name was Francis Wallace, and he was a writer, and he lived in Bellaire, and he was a graduate of Notre Dame. So, when Cy was recruited for Army, he immediately was going to make sure that he doesn't play against Notre Dame, and he was the one who looked all the stuff up…"

THE LETTER RECEIVED in the offices of Secretary of War Patrick Hurley leveled an explosive charge: that cadet Cyril Letzelter had falsified his application to the academy to conceal the fact that he was, in fact, over the statutory age of admission. His age was relevant because the cutoff for admission to the academy was 22 years of age. His official application had listed his birth date as August 8, 1907, showing him to be 21 years and 11 months old—one month shy of the cutoff for admissions.

If the August 1907 birth date were to be proven false, it meant that Cyril would not only have violated the rules of the institution, but in obtaining his appointment via fraudulent means, he would have clearly broken the law. The penalties for such an offense could be severe, not least of which would be his near-certain expulsion from West Point.

Based on the family history, this appears to have been a ticking time bomb waiting to explode for some time.

According to Cyril's sister, Betty Hamm, shortly after the public announcement of her brother's appointment in the summer of 1929, Rockne's trusted bird-dog, the Bellaire native

---

What is critical to note is that at the time of this interview, neither the writer nor Mrs. Hamm had any knowledge of who Wallace was, his importance as a sports fixer and writer, or the close relationship Wallace had with Knute Rockne. His role as one of Rockne's "bird-dogs" and as one of the famous coach's most trusted allies in the New York media was completely unknown to both. To Mrs. Hamm, he was just a writer and Notre Dame graduate from Bellaire who had an axe to grind because Cyril was from archrival Martins Ferry and had played a crucial part in two of the most embarrassing losses ever inflicted on Knute Rockne and the Notre Dame football program.

It was the writer's later discovery of Wallace's relationship with Rockne, exhaustively researched by Murray Sperber in *Shake Down the Thunder*, that led this writer to begin pulling on the different threads in order to reconstruct what actually happened. What is reported here is based on the best attempt to logically place Wallace's role, as known from family history, with the documented record still available.

Francis Wallace, began conducting research in Belmont and Monroe counties. Wallace's inquiries focused on determining the correct date of Cyril's birth. There is no evidence that Rockne asked Wallace to look into this question, nor is there any record of what prompted Wallace to begin looking. Most likely, with the Ohio Valley being made up of relatively small, close-knit communities, Wallace received a tip that Cyril's age was a subject that might bear investigating. It appears that same insular community fabric is what alerted the Letzelters that something was amiss.

In any case, over the next year, when Wallace was back in the region, he spent some time looking for official records that might confirm or rebut Cyril's date of birth. As a result of this process, Wallace apparently obtained damning evidence that Cyril had, in fact, falsified the birth date on his West Point application.

Most noteworthy were the records from the Monroe County courthouse in Woodsfield, Ohio, which can still be viewed there today. In the large, leather bound ledger from 1906–07, Cyril's birth is distinctly recorded on December 8, 1906, making him seven months over the legal age of admission when he reported to West Point in July of 1929.

Moreover, regardless of how later correspondence and news reports would explain the matter, there is no doubt that this had been a willful act. There was absolutely no confusion within Cyril's family regarding his actual date of birth, a fact underlined by his father's letter to him only months before the controversy, in December 1929, when he acknowledged Cyril's recent birthday.

That being the case, there is no clear indication that either Cyril's family or representatives of the Army had advance knowledge that he was misstating his date of birth to gain admission. It is almost certain, however, that Bud Mullaney knew.

In any event, it probably didn't take long for word to get around the region that Wallace was looking into Cyril's background. And once word got out, it wasn't long before both Mullaney and the family became thoroughly aware of the threat and quickly began to close ranks to protect Cyril and his reputation.

The first order of business was to produce a counter-narrative that would cast doubt on the suggestion that the December 1906 birth date was the actual birth date. They got some sloppy assistance from their friends in the Catholic Church.

Decades later, the newly ordained Rev. Thomas Hamm, Cyril's nephew, was assigned to the same, tiny St. Sylvester's Catholic Church in Woodsfield that Cyril had attended for mass and school and received his sacraments as a small child. The adjacent church cemetery to this day is a virtual Letzelter family tree, with dozens of Letzelters, Poultons, Schumachers, and others, all of whom have shared roots that stretch directly back to Schonau and the Black Forest region of modern Germany. It remains to this day a sort of "home base" for the Letzelter descendants of the Ohio Valley.

In 1930, the Rev. Gilbert Mehler had been the pastor of St. Sylvester's for little more than a year. However, before his arrival in Woodsfield, he had been assigned to parishes in Pittsburgh. He was also, according to Rev. Hamm, a sports fanatic, and he remembered Cyril well from his heroics at Carnegie Tech.

Priest or not, the good reverend apparently wasn't above a little bit of sinning when he felt it served the greater good. According to Hamm, it was Mehler himself who went into the official parish baptismal registers and doctored the record to show that Cyril's actual birth date was December 8, 1907. Both Hamm and the writer have viewed the doctored record, and the forgery is obvious. The register that recorded baptisms in chronological order throughout 1906 shows Cyril's baptism occurring on December 23. However, an added note in the extreme right-hand margin registers the addition of the year "1907." The notation in this manner is unique—no other record shows a year in this fashion. Cyril's baptismal record also rests right between the beginning of December 1906 and January 1907—right where one would expect a record from December 1906 to appear; whereas all other baptisms from December of 1907 are recorded pages later, after a full year of baptisms performed throughout 1907 in the parish.

Nevertheless, Mehler's help gave Cyril's allies a critical starting point. Much like the fictional courtroom dramas where the defense receives unexpected help from a man of the cloth willing to lend his unimpeachable credibility to the cause, Letzelter now had an unexpected and powerful ally from a source that was tricky to accuse publicly of misconduct.

Providing fodder for this confusing narrative was Cyril's family history. It was the passing of his mother, Mollie Poulton, when he was nine and his extended years living with his aunt and uncle, Laura and John Caton, that explained the family confusion around his birth date. As the story went, his father Michael had been traveling and apprenticing as a plumber for most of Cyril's life up until he moved to Martins Ferry. The exact date of his birth supposedly had been lost to memory. The differing records just went to prove that no one was certain when Cyril had been born. According to Cyril's boosters, it was all an honest mistake.

As best as can be determined, it was likely with this new proof in hand that Cyril's father Michael, at some point before the letter to Hurley, traveled personally to the Monroe County Courthouse to contest the official record showing Cyril was born in 1906. According to a contemporaneous news report from the *New York Evening Graphic*, Michael insisted instead that the correct date was December 8, 1907—matching the church's contention—and demanded that the courthouse change the official record. Additionally, other reporting indicated that Cyril's employment records from Wheeling Steel were also brought in to supplement his story—a clear indication that Mullaney had falsified additional documents to help protect his protégé.

Of course, the County Clerk was having none of it. Frankly, the mere idea of approaching legal authorities to demand the alteration official records is an indication of how concerned Cyril's family and supporters were becoming about the matter. It was a reckless move that very nearly had serious consequences.

One envisions a fairly rushed and chaotic effort coordinated behind the scenes by Mullaney, who had both Cyril's and his own reputation to protect. Nothing underscores this chaos more than the fact that, in working to build this counter-narrative, they had all ignored the actual August 1907 date Cyril had recorded on his application. By trying to focus on establishing a mistake in Cyril's birth year, they inadvertently created a potential third birth date for Cyril. While this certainly added to the confusion, it did not ultimately help their credibility.

THE ORIGINAL LETTER to Secretary Hurley has not been found. We only know of its existence because the *New York Evening Graphic* published its content and the date sent in late November 1930. However, absent a copy of the letter or some other evidence, it is impossible to ascertain who forwarded the allegations to the Department of War. However, common sense leads to some reasonable assumptions.

While that report did not include a copy of the original letter, it did produce a full photograph of the reply, signed personally by the adjutant general, and sent on behalf of Secretary Hurley. That response was dated October 6, 1930, and referenced the previous letter as being dated five days prior. Five days is a fast turnaround time and indicates that the original note, when received by the War Department, was quickly recognized as important and requiring prompt official acknowledgment. The obvious conclusion is that an individual of recognized importance either forwarded or signed the original correspondence.

It is hard to imagine that the War Department or West Point would just turn a blind eye to evidence that a cadet had falsified his way into the academy, especially given the clear evidence before the fall of 1930 that Cyril was not being shown any favoritism as all. And yet, after sending the reply, nearly seven weeks passed before the matter came to a head with little evidence the Army did anything to open either a formal or informal inquiry into the matter. In fact, Cyril continued to play every week as if nothing unusual was going on.

In short, the information suggests that the Army chose initially to treat the letter with professional respect while doing little to take the allegations seriously. When one considers that, and then factors in the very recent and heated battles between Congressman Hamilton Fish and the Secretary of War over player eligibility in the Army football program, it seems fairly reasonable to suspect that it was likely Fish himself who forwarded the allegations to the Army. In addition, the totality of how Army handled the public relations side of this controversy bore a striking resemblance to how it had handled Fish's earlier explosion over the case of Chris Cagle.

However, even if Fish was involved, where would he have come into this information? Again, one can only speculate, but it bears noting that while Francis Wallace hailed from the Ohio Valley, after his graduation from Notre Dame he went to work as a top sportswriter in New York. His location and his beat assignments, particularly his coverage of college football, would have given him ample opportunity to cross paths with New York Congressman Fish. Also, as a native of Martins Ferry's archrival Bellaire and as an alumnus of Notre Dame, even with damning information in his possession, Wallace would have difficulty filing a news story about the matter without having his individual biases called into question. This challenge would have been especially true if Wallace had uncovered the information on his personal initiative, rather than being assigned by an editor. Add the fact that the Letzelter camp had produced contradictory information of its own, backed by the word of a Catholic priest, and Wallace would almost certainly have needed a third party to help the story gain traction. Given Fish's long, high-profile role as an Army football critic, the match would have been obvious.

In any event, weeks passed without any apparent effort to investigate the matter by the academy. Cyril continued to play as part of the first team and continued to live up to the expectations that he was the heir to Chris Cagle on the gridiron. On October 18, Cyril played what might have been his best game for the academy in Boston, when the Army lined up against Hamilton Fish's beloved Harvard. Cyril played a key role in Army narrowly edging the Crimsons by a score of 6-0. Contemporary accounts told that his speed and skill at middle linebacker repeatedly thwarted Harvard's attempts to work the ball around the ends of the line, and he played a critical role in stopping a late drive into Army territory that could have been the difference in the game. There is no doubt that Fish would have noticed this, only adding to his motive to turn his ire toward Army and Letzelter.

With the War Department apparently dragging its feet on addressing the matter, and the all-important contest against Notre Dame looming on the schedule, there was an increasing motive for Wallace and others gunning for Cyril to pressure Army to take action.

What seems to have tipped the balance, however, was the anti-Letzelter camp obtaining a key new piece of evidence and turning to perhaps the most mendacious news outlet of that time operating in New York City, the *New York Evening Graphic*.

THE *NEW YORK Evening Graphic* was a short-lived, early forerunner to the now famous New York tabloid press. It was founded in 1924 by Bernarr Macfadden, a publisher and an early proponent of bodybuilding and nutritional health theories. Outside his work in publishing, he is considered to have been the predecessor of such famous fitness celebrities as Charles Atlas and Jack Lelane.

Macfadden launched the *Graphic* in the shadow of his other, more exploitative publishing ventures. The most notable example was *True Story*, the first of what became known as "confessions magazines," in which staff writers composed allegedly true anecdotes emphasizing topics that expanded the boundary of acceptable discourse. *True Story* was a forum for tales about premarital sex, illegitimacy, crime, and myriad other subjects not touched by the traditional media of the time.

The concept behind the *Graphic* was to apply a similar boundary-breaking ethos to the daily newspaper. And while the paper itself only lasted eight years, it laid the template for tabloid culture. Like modern tabloids, the *Graphic* emphasized large, splashy headlines, breathless scandal, and a groundbreaking use of art and photography to supplement the stories it reported. The paper also launched the careers of celebrity journalists Walter Winchell, Louis Sobol, and sportswriter and future variety-show host Ed Sullivan.

At the time, the general public was not quite ready for what Macfadden had to offer. By 1930 it had only been nine years since the first commercial radio broadcast station, KDKA in Pittsburgh, Pennsylvania, started airing daily. The primary source of news still arrived once a day, in the form of a newspaper. There simply wasn't enough bandwidth to support a media scandal culture—yet. Looking back with the perspective of our modern media culture, we can see that Macfadden's ideas clearly won out in the end, but at the time the public didn't want it, and his tabloid became derisively known as the *"porno-Graphic."* Understanding this media culture is important to understanding the context of Letzelter's decision to lie on his academy application and why the *Graphic* was uniquely positioned to play the role that it did.

Without excusing the falsification of his birth date, one can still see that given a lack of common knowledge of West Point application guidelines or easy access to public records, Cyril was likely encouraged by the low odds of discovery. Even if discovered, this was not normally the type of thing that landed in the hands of reporters and made for scandal.

Counterintuitively, it was its unconventional approach to news that made the *Graphic* the perfect tool for those working to pressure Army to take immediate action against Cyril. The story they had and the information they collected was unquestionably damning. But so long as there were grounds for dispute over the facts of the matter, and so long as Army was content to delay action, Cyril's opponents were left with few traditional options to press the subject. The *Graphic* and its cynical, unconventional, and boundary-breaking approach to the news was the perfect vehicle to break the deadlock. Its reputation all but ensured that once a reporter began asking pointed questions on the record, it was only going to be a matter of time before the tabloid would splash the story across its pages.

THERE IS NO way to discern exactly how long the *Graphic* was working on the story. It is certain is that, by November 3, the periodical had secured a letter from the Martins Ferry School District stating that when Cyril enrolled in the district for the first time in 1923, his birth date had been listed with the proper legal date: December 8, 1906. This new piece of evidence showed definitively that his family was aware of the correct birth date within six years of his applying to West Point.

This evidence helped put the lie to the idea that confusion reigned because he had been partially raised by the Catons and unsure of his actual birth date. Here was evidence that after Cyril had left the care of his relatives and reunited full-time with his father, the family was wholly aware of his correct birth date.

It was around this same time that sports pages across the country reported that Cyril had taken ill, was admitted to the academy infirmary, and was likely to miss the marquee game against Illinois to be played at Yankee Stadium in New York. One suspects his admission for medical care could have been an early indication that the growing storm of controversy was privately beginning to take a toll. However, at the last minute, Cyril apparently made an unexpected recovery and decided to make the trip to New York and play after all.

It was during this trip to New York City on Saturday, November 8, that two reporters from the *Graphic* set upon Cyril and presented him with the new evidence. He seems to have been caught completely by surprise. According to the *Graphic*,

> When Letzelter was given a chance to speak for himself, he made no mention of the belief that he was born August 8, 1907, as listed in the academy records. Nor did he deny the

evidence of the court record of his birth, merely saying that "he was never very sure about his age anyhow." He didn't, at the time, say anything about the August birth date on the academy records and, when the alteration of the parish records was brought to his attention, he accepted the fact without comment of any kind.

Finally, he tactically admitted that something reprehensible had happened somewhere. He did this by conceding that, if the documents became public, he would be forced to leave the academy.

Whether he realized it at that moment or not, Cyril Letzelter's football career was over. He would never suit up and play an organized game again.

THE STORY BROKE on the evening of Tuesday, November 18, when West Point Colonel Walter K. Wilson, the executive officer of the academy, released a statement to select media announcing that a heretofore unknown internal investigation revealed that Cyril was over the legal age when admitted to the academy in July of 1929. As a result, the authorities immediately barred him from playing any and all varsity sports. Just months after the Chris Cagle scandal, a new controversy had permanently benched his heir apparent.

By the following morning, the story was picked up by the wire services and was dominating the sports pages from coast to coast. The ordinarily staid *New York Times* even highlighted its reported piece as a special, exclusive report, as did its rival *New York Herald Tribune*.

Most important, however, was that the academy had apparently accepted Cyril's explanation at face value. Wilson stated that its investigation indicated that Cyril had acted "in absolute good faith" and noted that confusion over his birth date was due to the loss of his mother at age nine and his upbringing by an aunt and uncle. The academy also announced that, contrary to the statutory requirements for admission, Letzelter would still be allowed to remain at the school.

There seems little doubt that this was another attempt by Army to downplay an embarrassing incident and to control the media narrative, just as it did months earlier in the case of Chris Cagle. Despite the quiet controversy that had been raging behind the scenes since the beginning of October, if not sooner, there is no evidence that the Army conducted any investigation into Cyril before making this announcement. The available evidence guides to the conclusion that West Point, knowing that the *Graphic* was on the verge of publishing a punishing exposé, decided to get out ahead of the story by breaking the news on their own terms. In this regard, they were mostly successful.

Thursday's *Graphic* account, now almost two full days behind the main story, came loaded with explosive allegations and information. It was also basically ignored.

Getting scooped by Army's preemptive strike did not stop the *Graphic* from making its best attempt. In a copyrighted story splashed over two full pages, under the screaming headline "LETZELTER'S AGE KNOWN TO WAR DEPT. SIX WEEKS," the story switched the focus of the attack onto the War Department itself, making the case that not only was Cyril underage but that the War Department had dragged its feet in investigating the matter.

To supplement its case, the *Graphic* decorated the story first with a photograph of Cyril's baptismal record covering

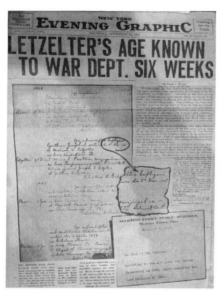

nearly half of page one, helpfully blowing up the portion showing the obvious forgery. The story also included images of Cyril's certified birth certificate from Monroe County, the letter from the Martins Ferry school district, and the letter of acknowledgment from the Army adjutant general both confirming receipt of allegations about Cyril's birth date and promising an investigation. It also,

The scandal over Cyril's eligibility for West Point gets the full-page, tabloid treatment from the *New York Evening Graphic* on November 20, 1930 — just days before he was to have a third crack at Knute Rockne's Notre Dame football team

tellingly, quoted liberally from Congressman Hamilton Fish, who provided a full written statement to include with the story.

The story itself was breathless in tone, and it went to great pains to suggest—not credibly—that it only decided to run the story after the Army claimed in its Tuesday release that the discrepancy in the birth dates was an honest mistake. To the *Graphic's* eye, this had been a willful attempt by the Army to cover up the real depth of Letzelter's deceit. The doctored baptismal record, as well as the paper's independent reporting of Michael Letzelter's attempt to get the Monroe County Clerk

238

to change the official legal record, stood as the most significant evidence pointing to a conspiracy.

The tone of the story notwithstanding, the reporting on the piece appears to have been solid. Cyril had lied on his application, the baptismal records were falsified, and his story of confusion over his actual birth date was simply not true. And it certainly appears accurate that the War Department took no significant steps to take action until the *Graphic* story seemed imminent.

Perhaps, had the *Graphic* been able to get the jump on Army and report its story first, the damage would have been greater. As it was, the story mostly faded from the sports pages a week and a half later, after the Cadets' matchup against Notre Dame on November 29.

A great deal of the coverage had emphasized the missing halfback, which is not surprising considering that Coach Sasse never hid the fact that he had been building his game plan around Cyril all season with an eye toward this matchup against Notre Dame. Sitting with the team on the sidelines in a contest he had once been destined to play, Cyril watched Army fall by the narrow score of 7-6. It is hard not to presume that, in such a close game, the outcome might have been different if Cyril had been allowed on the field.

For Francis Wallace, no doubt, it was a mission well accomplished. It was he who had gotten the ball rolling against Cyril, and his efforts had borne fruit just in time to prevent Letzelter from taking the field and having an opportunity to produce a potential third dramatic victory over Rockne.

As for Rockne himself, there is no surviving evidence that he was involved in or even aware of Wallace's efforts against Cyril. But there is no doubt he was keenly aware of what had happened to Cyril and how he had benefitted. The evidence comes from a newspaper account of an encounter between Letzelter and Rockne later in the season.

Unexpectedly, near the end of the season, the War Department got personally involved in the ongoing dispute between West Point and Annapolis. In light of the growing devastation of the Great Depression, the top brass ordered both academies to meet for a mid-December benefit game at Yankee Stadium, with the proceeds to going to unemployment relief. Cyril, as had been the case since he was ruled ineligible to play, traveled with the team to assist at Coach Sasse's request.

After the game Rockne himself, who had been in attendance providing commentary as part of the assembled media horde, decided to visit the Army locker room after the match. The first person he encountered as he entered the clubhouse was none other than Cyril himself. They approached each other and shook hands, and then Rockne, in a transparent reference to the recent scandal over Cyril's age, looked at him and asked him directly:

"Where's your grey hair?"

After the Fall

After an autumn of extreme turmoil and the abrupt, public and embarrassing end of his season and football career, the Christmas holidays undoubtedly offered the hope of respite for Cyril. His initial response to the threat from those looking to expose his secret had prevented his expulsion from the academy. However, events had occurred so quickly, and in such a state of crisis, that there had been little time for the twenty-three-year-old to reflect. The strategy to prevent the exposure of his secret had essentially locked him to a public commitment to remain a cadet regardless of his status as a football player. What was still unclear was whether this was actually his desire or just the side effect of a strategy that ultimately failed to preserve his ability to play ball.

The respite would not last long. Eight weeks later, the third major scandal in less than twelve months involving the Army program would erupt. It would drag Cyril back into the public light. And this time, it would bring a real investigation that would again threaten Cyril's ability to remain a cadet, would pull his friends and advocates into its web, and would divide the football-crazed citizens of the Ohio Valley.

NOT LONG AFTER the New Year, the *Providence Evening Bulletin* in Rhode Island carried its own copyrighted story claiming it had come into possession of an explosive letter. The letter, from W. T. Wrightman of New York—a member of the Army Athletic Association—was written to Kenneth Goff, a star football player for Rhode Island State who had been the second-highest scorer in the East during the recently completed season.

In his letter, Wrightman advised Goff to send a letter to Congressman George Stobbs of Rochester, Massachusetts, stating that he had been living in Stobbs's district for the past year with a former star and alumnus of West Point. The problem with this advice was that Goff, in fact, had not been living in the district at all.

The purpose of the letter Goff was directed to send was to falsely establish residency for the purpose of gaining an appointment. Damningly, in the same story, the alumnus flatly denied having sheltered Goff for the past year and publicly denied even knowing him. When pressed, Wrightman claimed his letter to Goff was written at the behest of the incoming cadet manager-elect for the coming 1931 Army football squad, Paul Carroll. So, unlike the previous controversies, this was an allegation of proselytizing that led directly to the staff of the Army football program.

It seems that Goff, like Letzelter, had his own fixer working to help him gain admission to West Point. Only in this case, instead of age eligibility, the challenge was one of residency. In both cases, the fixers and the would-be players had attempted to find a way around the rules and into West Point. An important difference in this case was that Goff's scheme was uncovered several months before official appointments would be made.

Recognizing the danger, the response from the congressman and the Army was swift. Stobbs quickly claimed Goff was denied a nomination due to his not having been a resident of his district, while the Army stated that a swift inquiry had shown that no one had helped Goff secure an appointment.

The fact that Goff never made it to West Point would seem to qualify this exposé as a minor one compared to the Cagle and Letzelter incidents. But those previous controversies had now focused more attention than ever on the recruitment of college stars to play at West Point. And, of course, as soon as the news broke, Congressman Hamilton Fish was coiled and ready for attack.

In a blistering statement released the next day, Fish tied the Goff incident directly to the Cagle and Letzelter scandals. Additionally, he called for an immediate investigation, stating, "The Goff case is just another one added to the Letzelter and Cagle cases, which prove there is something very wrong in regard to the status of amateur football at West Point."

If the fact that this was the third recruiting scandal to hit the program in under seven months weren't enough to spur the deep, internal inquiry Fish and so many others desired, they would receive unexpected help from a new figure on the scene who had a very deep commitment to West Point.

On November 21, 1930, the day after the *Graphic* ran its exposé on Letzelter and the War Department, the Army swore in a new chief of staff who received Fish's formal call for a new investigation. That new chief was already on his way to becoming a legend as the youngest major general in the United States Army. He was also a graduate and former superintendent of West Point. His name was Douglas MacArthur.

MacArthur seems to have taken the charges more seriously than anyone previously in a position to take action.

Fish made his request on January 29, and MacArthur immediately tasked the adjutant general of West Point, Lt. Col Sherborne Whipple, with conducting an investigation.

In less than five days, Whipple had drafted and sent separate and formal letters of inquiry to Cyril's father, his aunt and uncle, and J. F. Mullaney with a series of pointed questions. While Whipple's letter itself is lost, the responses by all parties remain, and they clearly state the questions Whipple had raised. In the case of the Letzelters and the Catons, they received letters requesting a response to four identical questions:

> *In what year did your son/nephew first learn that Dec. 8, 1906, was not his true birthday?*
>
> *What caused him to have doubt as to his correct age?*
>
> *Did he ever discuss his age with you? If so, when, and what was said?*
>
> *Did you ever hear him say anything about being too old to enter the Military Academy? If so, what?*

Given what was already known, these were fairly standard questions. And the replies from both were as one would expect from family attempting to protect Cyril. They stuck to their original story and claimed the whole affair was a mix-up born of confusion stemming from the loss of Cyril's mother.

Of far greater concern was the letter Whipple sent to Mullaney, where he clearly indicated that the Army was investigating specific allegations that there had been attempts to falsify birth records on Cyril's behalf, both at St. Sylvester's Church and with the Clerk of Monroe County. Whipple appears to have referenced an allegation that came into his possession only recently as part of the direction to reopen the inquiry. That new allegation came in the form of a statement written shortly after West Point removed Cyril from the team in mid-November. Likely because by that time the matter was considered closed, it apparently had not been forwarded to the academy for follow-up until Congressman Fish demanded the new inquiry.

The statement, made by a Moundsville brick factory executive named Allen B. Adams, claimed that he had "obtained a confession from the party that was guilty of the attempted change in birth records," and pointed the finger squarely at Mullaney. Without the full letter from Whipple or the specific statement from Adams—both of which are lost to time—it cannot be ascertained whether Adams incorrectly accused Mullaney of personally attempting to change the birth records, or if he correctly accused Mullaney of masterminding the cover-up. In either case, what is clear is that Mullaney, smartly, chose in his response to assume the former, and moved quickly and powerfully to impeach Adams's credibility.

Upon receiving the letter from Whipple, Mullaney immediately wired a telegram to Lt. Col. Whipple that read as follows:

"WE ARE GETTING SOME PLACE ON MR. A. I WOULDN'T KNOW THE MAN IF I SAW HIM. NONE OF MY CLERKS KNOW HIM. HE HAS CALLED ME SEVERAL TIMES ON THE PHONE. DON'T EVEN KNOW THE PRIEST AT WOODFIELD. WAS NEVER IN HIS CHURCH OR HIS HOME. INTEND TO SEE MR. A. ON MONDAY WITH AN ATTORNEY.

J.F. MULLANEY

There is little doubt that Mullaney had been handling the family's response to the crisis from the very beginning. He was fully aware of the letters sent to the Letzelters and Catons, and he personally sent copies of their official replies to Cyril before sending them to the academy investigators. It seems fair to assume that whatever steps Michael Letzelter took back in Woodfield, if not Mullaney's explicit suggestion, were certainly undertaken with Mullaney's awareness and consent. And now, with his telegram, Mullaney revealed the key points of his strategy.

Simply put, he was ignoring the inference that he had been the driver of the cover-up and instead focusing on the specific allegations that he had been personally involved in the modification of birth records. Because Mullaney had not undertaken these tasks personally, he was able not only to deny the charges but to respond with outrage and even threaten Adams with legal action.

Shortly after sending his telegram to Whipple, Mullaney then dashed off a quick, handwritten letter to Cyril explaining everything that had occurred, describing the telegram sent to Whipple, and detailing exactly how he and his family planned to respond. Then, as good his word, Mullaney and his attorney met face-to-face with Adams.

The meeting occurred on the evening of February 9 in the law office of Walter McGlumphy in the Mercantile Banking and Trust Company in Moundsville, West Virginia. The only description of the meeting is contained in Mullaney's follow-up letter to Whipple the next day. However, while Mullaney's version is obviously one-sided, it seems clear that his intent was to fully communicate the legal threat Adams faced if he did not retract his story. Mullaney described the meeting as follows:

> *After explaining the matter thoroughly to Mr. McGlumphy, he stated that some proceeding could be taken against A. B. Adams for placing the statements above on record in the War Department when they were untrue. At 8:00 p.m. Adams came in. This was the first time I had ever seen him. He went on with great blustering talk as all would be reformers do. Then when we asked him why he made such statements about me knowing they were untrue, he stated that the only thing he took and considered a confession from me, was when I had told him over the phone some months ago that the Army had never influenced Cyril Letzelter to enter West Point. Of course, you can see that this was a silly cover up and had nothing to do with the points set forth in the two paragraphs. But he insisted he had no other idea in mind when he made the statements.*

In Mullaney's version, what he claims he and Adams discussed months before is completely noncontroversial. Even the most aggressive reinterpretation would not point to any

247

wrongdoing whatsoever. And yet, according to Whipple, Adams clearly did claim that Mullaney was the party that "was guilty of the attempted changes in the birth records." One cannot resolve the exact facts of the charges and counter-charges. What is obvious, however, is that Mullaney's gambit was to intimidate Adams into backing off his claims. Although only Mullaney's version of events survives, it seems the gambit was successful.

THE LETTERS IN response to the Whipple inquiry were all returned on February 10, 1931, and became part of a growing mass of evidence compiled for an official board of review. Neither the Cagle case nor the first investigation into Letzelter's birth date had merited the creation of such a panel. Its existence speaks to both the lax response to the charges when initially leveled and the change in approach that occurred after the allegations of the Goff incident and the appointment of MacArthur as chief of staff.

The Board of Review was comprised of three senior officers at the academy: Col. Clayton Wheat, professor of English; Col. A. G. Gillespie, professor of ordnance and gunnery; and Col. H. Leukemia, professor of economics and history. In addition to the inquiry performed by Col. Whipple, the panel also ordered the Army coach, Ralph Sasse, to travel back to Woodsfield to examine firsthand all the available records.

It was at this time that Cyril was assigned formal representation from the office of the Judge Advocate General. According to his sister, the JAG officer advised him that as part of his defense, he was to make no mention of football and state that his sole ambition in coming to West Point was "to become an officer and a gentleman."

Based on the surviving correspondence, Sasse's involvement in the investigation was advantageous for Cyril. Not only was he the coach who had attempted to build his new Army team around Cyril, but it was clear that the entire affair, and the burden it had created for Cyril, had caused him great distress. He later wrote Mullaney, "I was very much worried about the entire affair as the boy has suffered enough, and additional newspaper publicity is only just that much more of a burden for the youngster to bear."

Fortunately for Cyril, when the results of the second inquiry were finally announced on May 1, it barely merited notice in the newspapers. The final report, issued by Major William Smith, superintendent of the academy, found that "not one scintilla of evidence was produced indicating that Cadet Letzelter has been guilty of fraud or had knowingly and with intent to deceive, misrepresented his age." However, it also formally found that his true date of birth was, in fact, December 8, 1906, making him 6 months and 23 days over the legal admission age. The decision of the academy mirrored the decision from the previous fall: Cyril would be allowed to remain at the academy and would still be barred from participating in athletics.

After eight months of turmoil, the Letzelter scandal at West Point had finally ended.

Beyond the Golden Age

By 1930 football had achieved a point of maturity. Countless new stadiums dotted the landscape. New conferences were born. The number of competitive programs exploded. The reach of the game grew with the popularity of radio broadcasts and extensive newspaper coverage of the sport. And, for the first time since the game's inception, the rules on the field were mostly settled. A contest viewed in 1931, excepting the size of the players and the style of equipment, is roughly the same as one sees today.

In hindsight, one thing that stands out about the Army football scandals of 1930–31 is that public condemnation grew from the act of recruiting itself. Whether it was Chris Cagle resigning from the academy, Cyril Letzelter falsifying his birth date to attend, or Kenneth Goff attempting to fabricate his place of residence to gain an appointment, in every case the common irritant to the reformers of the era was that proselytizing for football talent occurred at all. The means of recruitment were more an afterthought.

This perspective of the era owed much to the fact that, since the inception of the Intercollegiate Athletic Association (the precursor to the modern National Collegiate Athletic Association) at the turn of the century, that body viewed the very act of recruiting as against the rules. Of course, because the association had no enforcement authority, the programs ignored the body's directives and provided all manner of incentives to potential players outside public view.

This perspective on recruiting began to change in 1935 when the five-year-old Southeastern Conference (SEC) voted to allow its schools to openly pay tuition, room, and board for their athletes. This move was obviously controversial, and the Big Ten and the leadership of the new NCAA moved quickly to condemn the decision. But the governing body was still powerless to stop the practice.

The NCAA took its first steps to address reality in 1948 with the passage of the Sanity Code. The measure for the first time allowed schools to pay tuition for athletes and permitted coaches to recruit for talent off campus. Room and board costs were still prohibited. The NCAA further threatened the expulsion of any schools that violated the code. Although viewed at the time as an insufficient half-measure, it marked the first open acknowledgment by the governing body that recruiting was here to stay.

Over time the NCAA position continued to evolve, and the association eventually added staff, refined rules, and created an enforcement arm that now exercises near total authority over matters related to recruitment. Oversight now tends to focus on what types of financial support for players are deemed acceptable. Tuition, room, and board are accepted; other types of financial incentive are not. But since the mid-1930s the act of recruitment itself has been broadly accepted.

When one considers that neither the Cagle, Letzelter, nor Goff affairs involved offering a financial incentive to play sports, it's entirely possible that had the Army recruitment scandals of 1930–31 happened just a few years later, they might not have become scandals at all.

IN LATE 1930, with the Great Depression raging and unemployment soaring, college football programs across the country began scheduling extra "charity" games to direct revenues toward various unemployment relief funds. As the most famous and controversial rivals of the era, it wasn't long before pressure began to build for an Army-Navy contest for such purpose. Humanitarian impulses notwithstanding, neither of the academies leaped at the idea.

However, as the end of the season drew near, the pressure grew. Representatives from both Illinois and New York made strong pitches to the Hoover administration for the hosting of such a game. One estimate claimed a contest could net as much as $750,000 for charitable purposes. Grudgingly, the academies began to negotiate, but they immediately got hung up on the same thorny issues of player eligibility.

Finally, the leadership of the War Department stepped in. Undoubtedly recognizing that the ongoing argument between West Point and Annapolis looked especially ridiculous in contrast to the philanthropic motives behind the potential contest, the brass ordered the academies to play at Yankee Stadium on December 13, 1930. It was the same game where Rockne and Cyril met in the Army locker room and the legendary coach taunted Cyril for his recent troubles regarding his age.

Seventy thousand fans came out to watch Army narrowly defeat Navy 6-0 in a game that raised $600,000 in revenues for the Salvation Army's unemployment relief efforts. It was such a success that the teams met again for the same purpose in 1931, this time before seventy-five thousand. At this point, having broken the cold war raging between the two institutions, and recognizing that the popularity of the game was such that ending play again was untenable, the academies began scheduling regular season contests again, with each team accepting the other's right to set their own eligibility guidelines.

In 1939, Army finally adopted the three-year eligibility rule.

AS THE BATTLE between the service academies finally began to fade in 1931 and the challenges of the Great Depression grew, Hamilton Fish's crusade against West Point football faded. As the economic crisis wore on, high-profile battles over college sports undoubtedly seemed more and more trivial. Besides, for Fish, there were bigger battles to fight, chiefly against his one-time political mentor, Franklin Delano Roosevelt.

As Roosevelt became president in 1933, Fish emerged as one of the loudest, most active voices against him. He became the ranking Republican on the House Rules Committee, where he led his party's efforts in opposing FDR's New Deal and America's increasing involvement in World War II. The same tenacious fury he had once focused on West Point he now aimed at the president, and it annoyed the ordinarily gregarious president to no end. FDR eventually banned Fish from White House and even incorporated him by name as part of a memorable refrain whereby the president regularly denounced his detractors as "Martin, Barton, and Fish."

Fish, like most Americans, dropped his opposition to World War II after Pearl Harbor and even suggested he might volunteer to fight, even though he was fifty-one years old at the time. He is remembered as one of the most strident anticommunists of his era.

In the 1944 election, as Roosevelt cruised to his historic fourth term via a national Democratic landslide, Fish lost his seat. He then retired from public life. He died in 1991 at the age of 102.

IN 1930, FRANCIS Wallace published his first book, *Huddle*, a story of college football based on Knute Rockne and Notre Dame. He eventually went on to write the hotly anticipated "Pigskin Preview" every year for decades, first for the *Saturday Evening Post* and later for *Collier's*. He also became a radio sports commentator for CBS and ABC.

He eventually went on to write seventeen books, most notably *Kid Galahad* in 1936, one of the few he wrote that were not football related. He also wrote, as one would expect, an early biography of his friend and mentor, Rockne. He was eventually able to successfully convert several of his stories into screenplays, including two versions of *Kid Galahad*, the latter of which starred Elvis Presley.

He was also one of the earliest and most vocal proponents for paying college athletes. He saw early on that colleges and universities were generating tremendous revenue for their schools, and he felt that it was an injustice that the same athletes making this wealth possible went largely uncompensated. Around mid-century, he even raised the issue with the legendary Walter Byers, the man who created the modern NCAA, pitching him on the idea of "tying a fixed rate of pay to the time a boy spends in practicing for and playing in college athletics." Byers, of course, rejected that idea at the time, but even he eventually came around to recognizing the unfairness for college athletes in the system he created.

Long after the passing of Rockne, it was said that Wallace continued to help working-class kids from the Ohio Valley attend and play football for the University of Notre Dame. He died in August of 1977 at the age of eighty-three.

FOR JOHN FRANCIS Mullaney, Cyril's collegiate football career appears to have been one of his last major projects, and perhaps his most successful. He mostly disappeared from public view after the abrupt end of Cyril's playing career, except occasionally appearing in print when sending tidbits to local sports reporters about the latest military assignment for his one-time protégé.

In the fall of 1938, just five years after Cyril graduated from West Point, Mullaney took ill with a kidney ailment and was eventually hospitalized for over six weeks before his health gave out. He died on November 22, 1938, in Martins Ferry, leaving a wife and two daughters. Perhaps ironically, newspaper accounts of his death could not seem to agree if he was sixty-one or sixty-three years old.

THREE MONTHS AFTER his meeting with Cyril in the Army locker room at Yankee Stadium, Knute Rockne wrapped up a visit with his sons in Kansas City, who were attending the Pembroke County Day School. He boarded a flight bound for Los Angeles where he was to participate in the production of the film *The Spirit of Notre Dame*. A little over an hour after takeoff, the plane, a Fokker F-10 Trimotor, experienced a catastrophic malfunction that caused the wings to separate from the hull. Rockne and seven others died when the plane crashed into a wheat field just outside of Bazaar, Kansas. In a macabre coincidence, it fell to Rockne's old friend Jesse Harper—the same former Notre Dame athletic director who had saved the football program from Ned Yost's Western Conference boycott, who also was now living in retirement only a hundred miles from the crash site—to identify Rockne's body.

At the time of his death, he had coached only four games in the brand-new stadium erected to accommodate the growth of the program he had built. It is still known as "the House that Rockne Built."

Of his twelve lifetime losses, Rockne lost only one game at home: the 1928 game against Carnegie Tech where Cyril Letzelter played the game of his life and was awarded the game ball.

The Colonel

ONE CAN EASILY divide the life of Cyril Letzelter into two parts; the periods before and after the public scandal that ended his football career. Before the scandal, Cyril's life was defined by football. After the scandal, his life was defined by his commitment to the military. In both parts, he achieved tremendous success, and in both parts, a promising future was suddenly and surprisingly cut short.

Upon reflection, it's important to remember that by the time the investigatory board issued its final decision on Cyril's future in May 1931, the Letzelter affair had been a full-blown crisis for eight consecutive months. Furthermore, that crisis had come fast on the heels of Cyril's tumultuous first year, where he nearly washed out of the academy due to poor grades. Outside of the fact that he had continued to advance as a student, one could easily describe Cyril's first two years at the academy as catastrophic. As late as May 1931, Coach Ralph Sasse was only cautiously optimistic that Cyril would stay with the academy as a cadet.

And yet Cyril developed a deep, fierce bond with the Army. It wasn't just a career to him; it became a calling. And that begs a question: How did a twenty-three-year-old man who experienced such incredible disappointment and public humiliation during his formative time at the academy develop such an enduring commitment to the values of West Point and the military?

CYRIL NEVER RETURNED to the Ohio Valley to live. Regardless of controversy and heartache, he took the "shining opportunity" once described by J. F. Mullaney and rode it away from the coal mines and steel mills into a better future, and he never looked back.

He received his commission as a second lieutenant upon

Cyril Joseph Letzelter, West Point Class of 1933

his graduation from West Point on June 13, 1933. Later that same day he married his incredibly patient and loving high school sweetheart, Ethel Williams. After a summer respite, they shipped out to Vancouver Barracks, just outside Portland, Oregon, where he stayed for the next six years, serving under the command of then-Brigadier General George Catlett Marshall, who went on to become the architect of the famous Marshall Plan to rebuild postwar Europe. From the time he left the academy until the outbreak of World War II, Cyril returned to West Point every autumn to assist in coaching Army football.

In 1936, he and Ethel welcomed their first daughter, Mary Elizabeth, named after Cyril's own mother whom he had lost two decades before. Two years later they had a second child, Lucille Ann, and then quickly shipped out to Fort Benning, Georgia, so Cyril could attend the United States Military Infantry Training School. Upon completion, now a first lieutenant, he was detailed back to West Point full time, where he joined the athletic department and added baseball and track to his coaching responsibilities. In 1940, his third and youngest child was born in New York State, a son, Cyril Joseph II.

With the onset of World War II, he moved his family to Omaha, Nebraska, near his old high school friend and now

Cyril Letzelter and his wife Ethel, leave the chapel on their wedding day — June 13, 1933 — the same day he graduated from West Point

brother-in-law, Kenneth Williams. He then headed to the European Theater of Operations. He arrived in Normandy two weeks after D-Day, where he was severely wounded in action and was awarded the Bronze Star and the Purple Heart. After a month of hospitalization, he returned to the front and saw battle for five consecutive months, including the Battle of the Bulge, while serving as a battalion commander.

By the end of the war, he had achieved the rank of lieutenant colonel, and he later served two consecutive tours in postwar Germany in the offices of the European Command, first as the branch chief for Army Intelligence and later as the commanding officer for the 7997th Composite Group. He returned to the American mainland in mid-1953 and continued to advance through the ranks, eventually returning to the place of one of his greatest triumphs.

THE REVEREND ROBERT Woodward, who oversaw, among other things, Notre Dame's Office for Military Affairs, prepared to greet his new faculty member assigned by the United States Army to run the university's ROTC program. As they met, with a smile and just the slightest hint of seriousness, he welcomed the middle-aged, uniformed man while reminding him that his heroic exploits against the legendary Knute Rockne and the Fighting Irish in 1926 and 1928 were not forgotten. He looked Colonel Cyril Letzelter in the eye and said to him, "Colonel, it took us twenty-five years before we would agree to even let you back on this campus." They shared a laugh.

According to surviving family, Cyril's billet at Notre Dame was one of the most satisfying posts of his career. While he had held his share of bureaucratic posts, he always preferred assignments that provided the opportunity to be a leader of other young men. He was a bit disappointed when the time came for him to withdraw from Notre Dame to attend the Army War College in Carlisle, Pennsylvania.

As he left, he penned a letter that summed up the importance that the University of Notre Dame, the Army, and his Catholic faith had come to represent in his adult life. Written on July 30, 1956, the letter appears to have been drafted and sent to prospective recruits for the ROTC program at the university. It sums up the arc of Cyril's life and the values that defined him, and it bears reprinting here:

> *As a Catholic and as an Army Officer with better than 25 years' experience I would like to call your attention to a matter of grave concern. I would like your assistance in ameliorating*

a condition which affects not only the good of the Army and of the Nation, but especially of the Church itself.

There is a serious lack of Catholic leadership in the Armed Services. Although we Catholics have done more than our share in filling up the ranks of the enlisted services, still we have never met our quota of commissioned officers. Nor do I believe that Notre Dame is doing her best when only one out of four of her graduates is accepting the responsibilities of military leadership. There are other Catholic Colleges that do better, having only one of the armed services.

I submit that no student of Notre Dame can assume any extracurricular activity that will pay off so liberally on the day of graduation, as a commission obtained via the ROTC. An Army ROTC student assumes no added liabilities, he serves no longer, and no sooner than the draftee. Yet his status is infinitely superior and more on the level with the reputation of this university. He has the freedom of financial independence. He is able to marry when he will, and support a family. He can determine in what capacity and with what associates he will serve. Above all, as an educated Catholic, he can have some impact on the life and culture of this nation.

It is with these thoughts in mind that I am sending you the enclosed brochure. This letter is mailed on the eve of my departure. I leave with great regret, and I close this letter and my assignment here by saying that the Army and the Nation needs more men of the high character and caliber of those trained at Notre Dame.

Sincerely,

C. J. Letzelter

Colonel, Infantry

Cyril Letzelter, a man of proud German descent, came of age in an America where his heritage was a stark liability and

his Catholic upbringing a ready invitation to bigotry. And yet, three decades later, he implored the students of the most famous Catholic institution in America to not only embrace patriotism but to pledge themselves to serving their nation. In a way, this triumph stands taller than any success he had decades

Colonel Cyril Joseph Letzelter I

before on the gridiron.

By the summer of 1957, he had successfully attended the Army War College in Carlisle, Pennsylvania, and had been requested for assignment to the Pentagon to serve as the executive officer for the Army's Assistant Chief of Staff for Intelligence. He had completed his annual physicals and was anticipating an expected promotion to brigadier general appropriate to his new billet.

It was not to be. On the afternoon of Sunday, July 27, while playing golf with friends, he fell ill and returned home.

Alarmed, his wife Ethel called for an ambulance. He never made it to the hospital. He died en route of a heart attack. He was only fifty-one years old.

Today, Colonel Cyril Joseph Letzelter looks over the nation's capital and the place of his last military post from atop a hill at his final resting place in Arlington National Cemetery.

AFTER CYRIL'S DEATH, his friend and eulogist, Brigadier General Charlie Rich, wrote of Cyril as an exceedingly rare alumnus of West Point who, unlike most who attended the academy, had achieved the status of being a legend while he was still a cadet. So the question remains: how did Cyril, whose first two years at the academy were so publicly painful and difficult, eventually become such a "legend"?

One cannot say with certainty when Cyril decided to stick it out at the academy or why he ultimately made the decision to stay. But what seems undeniable is that a great deal of his commitment stemmed from the fact that, under tremendous pressure to take action and expel him from the academy, the Army instead stuck by his side and supported him during what was unquestionably the most wrenching period of his life to date. It is through such crucibles that one makes lifelong bonds. Such was likely the case here.

For example, though banned from participating in varsity athletics as a player, Coach Sasse quickly made it clear to Cyril that his team would not abandon him. After allowing him on the sidelines in the days after being removed from the roster, Sasse continued to keep Cyril with the team, traveling for all the games and allowing him to help in any way he could,

263

short of taking the field. By the following spring, Sasse informed Cyril's mentor, Bud Mullaney, of his most unusual plan to try to use Cyril as a coach for the 1931 season despite his status as a cadet—a radical idea given that such roles were reserved for the faculty. And in this, perhaps we see the gift that gave Cyril the strength to continue, and persevere, in the face of embarrassment and disappointment.

Like most institutions of higher learning, the annual yearbooks at West Point reserve a special section for graduating seniors providing a brief listing of their activities while attending. The entry under Cyril's name in the spring of 1933 is unnaturally short, as his sporting pursuits could only list the brief time before his disqualification from play. And yet his entry contains something wholly unique. A single word apparently never listed before, or since, as a student activity for a cadet at West Point:

"Coach"

Afterword

September 2, 2016—Martins Ferry, Ohio

NINETY-ONE YEARS after his graduation, Cyril J. Letzelter is being inducted into the Martins Ferry High School Athletics Hall of Fame. If it seems overdue, one must take into consideration that, for all the community's love for athletics— and football in particular—the Hall of Fame was only created two years prior.

A group of surviving family members have made the trip back to the old mill town to participate in the events and accept the honor on behalf of the long-passed Cyril. Included are two of his surviving children, Lucy and Cyril II, several grandchildren and great-grandchildren, and most notably, his ninety-one-year-old surviving half-sister, Betty Hamm, who has been transported from a nearby assisted living facility to take part in the occasion.

It's the beginning of Labor Day weekend in Martins Ferry, and the Purple Riders are preparing for their first home football game of the season

The weather is surprisingly mild. One of the hottest summers in memory seems to have broken. The skies are clear, the humidity is light, and a pleasant breeze makes the air comfortable.

Coming into the community, one views the reminders of the past economic power of the Ohio Valley everywhere. The riverfront that stretches from Bellaire to Steubenville is littered with once proud, now shuttered steel mills. Rather than

265

advertising their brand, they instead advertise the vast facilities and lands now available for lease.

The homes stacked up on the western banks of the Ohio River rise in elevation on streets systematically cut from the hillside, each at higher elevation. The hills to the west, the river to the east, and the zig-zag nature of the streets induce a sense of claustrophobia that has likely been present since the community's earliest days.

The houses themselves, never fancy, show the signs of age and wear. Roofs sag, paint has faded, windows are boarded. But on many, American flags fly, and just as often, signs and flags pledging allegiance to the Purple Riders of Martins Ferry.

The Charles R. Shreve High School building has been abandoned now for newer academic facilities situated on a nearby hilltop, where one is treated to breathtaking views down into the great Ohio River Valley.

But the football field remains exactly where it has been for over nine decades, along the riverfront on the old Carmichael property. The original brick-and-mortar grandstand still stands, showing the wear of time. Across the field, a newer, more modern aluminum-and-steel grandstand supplements the older portion that still sits on the home side of the field. Everywhere one sees the pride of the Purple Riders— from the working-class man standing near the entrance of the grandstand, conducting an audible running dialogue with himself over each play on the field, to the worried mothers, hands over their mouths, silently praying after witnessing a particularly vicious tackle from the safety of their seat, to the younger children running around the grandstands wearing football jerseys of their own, playing with friends, and begging for money to spend on treats from the concession stand.

The decades have gone by. The community has changed. Many of the jobs have disappeared. But the pride remains. The people of Martins Ferry, as they always have been, are out in full force to support their team—to support the continuing promise of high school football.

They are here. Dreaming.

Dreaming of heroes.

Author's Note

If my eldest son had never gotten his learner's permit to drive, I never would have gotten to meet my grandfather. I'll explain:

You see, I never really got to know my grandparents. I was only seven when my fraternal grandmother, the only one I recall meeting, died. While I grew up with friends who talked about or visited their grandparents, I had to be satisfied with the memories passed down to me by my parents.

The most vivid memory I recall from my childhood about Grandpa Letzelter had nothing to do with his time as an athlete or as a soldier. Rather, it was a story my mother often told about how other young kids in the neighborhood would come to the Letzelter home, knock on the door, and ask if her dad could come out and play. The story almost always ended with my mom telling me how much her dad loved kids, and how much I would have loved meeting him.

Unfortunately, he died very young of a heart attack, just a few months after my mom and dad got married. So instead of experiences, I got second-hand memories.

Even so, when it came to my Grandfather Letzelter, as a young child I knew him described mostly as "the Colonel" because of his career as a military officer in the Army. His exploits as a football player came up only in passing. And for the most part, I found those stories confusing. There was a tale of how he had scored in a game against Knute Rockne and got the game ball. I, of course, would ask about the ball, only to told that it had been returned to Carnegie Tech years before. (In truth, as I discovered in researching this book, it had actually been given to his old high school in Martins Ferry, where it remains on display today.) Sending the game ball back to Carnegie was hard for preadolescent me to grasp. My dad was a proud alumnus of Notre Dame, and as a family, we were all big fans. I could never get the logic of sending the game ball from a Notre Dame game to anywhere other than Notre Dame.

The first time I can remember honestly grasping this significance of my grandfather's college football exploits from the 1920s was in September of 2007 when tiny Appalachian State upset the number-five-ranked Michigan Wolverines in football. It is inarguably one of the biggest upsets in the history of college football, but its occurrence led to a brief run of stories about other great upsets of the game. Nearly every list included the Notre Dame–Carnegie Tech contest of 1926 at or near the top.

But even this did not drive the point home until my mom pointed out that 1926 game being talked about in the news was the same one in which her father had played. I remain embarrassed to admit that the revelation left me dumbstruck. How could I not have known this?

The short answer is that my mother, like her father and siblings, don't like to brag. Fortunately, I am in many ways my father's son, and thus, as an Irish loudmouth, I rarely feel constrained by such manners.

As it happens, that revelation coincided with my growing interest in genealogy. Having majored in history in college, I found that digging into all of this stuff helped scratch an old itch. But I never dug too deep into this particular story until 2013.

That was the year my oldest son, Justin, got his learner's permit. Heading into the summer, I came up with the idea of taking him on a road trip to give him a chance to do some serious driving with me, so we went east to do some genealogy research on both the Grady and Letzelter families, both of whom have deep roots in Ohio.

Long story short, the trip, which we launched with a barely planned itinerary and no certain end date, resulted in us driving all the way to West Glover, Vermont, to see my aunt Lucille Smith, my mother's younger sister. I knew she had interesting family history tidbits I might like to see, and continuing to Vermont didn't seem that much farther than we had already travelled from Illinois to western Pennsylvania (I said I liked history, not geography!).

Well, she didn't just have historical tidbits. When she showed me the vast amount of information she had on my grandfather, I suspect my jaw hit the floor. When I left Vermont that week, the trunk of my car overflowed with a priceless collection of scrapbooks, newspapers, letters, army records, ticket stubs, and old photographs stretching back to Cyril Letzelter's first steps onto a high school gridiron.

I decided to write this book for a very simple reason. The more I poured through this information and then supplemented it with research of my own, the more thunderstruck I was with the story of my grandfather. It was too much to remember, and too much to tell someone verbally. Almost for the sake of my own sanity, I felt that it needed to be written down.

What you are holding right now was written for my family, plain and simple. If you are reading this and are not a member of my family, it's because of them and a few of my closest friends. They have convinced me, as I have shared my progress with them over time, that others might enjoy this story as well.

Of course, I have some people I want to thank for their ongoing support. First and foremost, I need to thank my aunt Lucille Smith and uncle Cyril Letzelter II. Both of them, along with my mother, have provided the vast majority of primary source research materials that allowed me to reconstruct this story. Without their generosity in entrusting me with this material, much of it close to a century old, this project would have been impossible.

On that 2013 trip across the northeastern America, we stopped to (unsuccessfully) find the game-day football supposedly returned to Carnegie Tech all those years before. While there, we were treated to the kindness of Mr. Terry Bodnar, the longtime defensive coordinator of the Carnegie Mellon Tartans. He also helped connect us with Kathleen Berman of the Carnegie Mellon University Archives, who opened up their files and could not have been more helpful.

I also need to thank the staff of the National Archives, the Archives of University of Notre Dame, and the Archives of the United States Military Academy at West Point. All of these outlets helped provide critical pieces that helped complete the puzzles of my grandfather's past.

All of my friends who provided encouragement over the past few years have my most sincere and lifelong thanks. There are too many of you to list.

Of course, I must thank my mom, and Mollie Poulton's namesake, Mary Elizabeth "Molly" Grady. Had she not planted that seed of interest about my grandfather all those years ago, I would not have had the curiosity or the drive to see this project through to the end. My desire to complete this work for her is the only reason that I, a serial procrastinator if ever there was one, got this done.

Finally, thanks to my family, especially my wife, Alyson. For over twenty-seven years she has suffered from my obsessions, and none has been bigger than this. She tolerated my weeks-long research trips without complaint and provided total encouragement. And I will not try to count the number of household "honey do's" that I delayed because I camped in front of a computer or a pile of old scrapbooks trying to discover something new. More importantly, she is by best friend and the love of my life, and for that alone, she has my eternal gratitude.

Michael Grady
Springfield, Illinois, August 2019

About the Author

Michael Grady is the 6th grandchild of Cyril Joseph Letzelter, and the youngest of Cyril's oldest child, Mary Elizabeth (Letzelter) Grady and her husband, the late W. Justin Grady.

He earned his degree in History in 1992 at Eastern Illinois University. Since then, he's worked in the field of state government relations. Since 2010, he's operated his own consulting firm where he works on issues supporting various local government bodies, advocating for public health and anti-tobacco policies, supporting the developmentally and intellectually disabled, and waste management and recycling.

He is an avid college football fan, and despite his love for his Grandfather's exploits against Knute Rockne, he remains a rabid fan of the Fighting Irish of Notre Dame, and still believes they got screwed out of the National Championship in 1989.

He lives in Springfield, Illinois with his wife Alyson and their three children; Justin, Aidan and Clare.